SOLUTIONS FOCUSED
SPECIAL EDUCATION

by the same editor

Restorative Practice and Special Needs
A Practical Guide to Working Restoratively with Young People
Nick Burnett and Margaret Thorsborne
ISBN 978 1 84905 543 7
eISBN 978 0 85700 968 5

of related interest

The Neurodiverse Classroom
A Teacher's Guide to Individual Learning Needs and How to Meet Them
Victoria Honeybourne
ISBN 978 1 78592 362 3
eISBN 978 1 78450 703 9

Creative Ideas for Solution Focused Practice
Inspiring Guidance, Ideas and Activities
Judith Milner and Steve Myers
ISBN 978 1 78592 217 6
eISBN 978 1 78450 497 7

Autism and Solution focused Practice
Els Mattelin and Hannelore Volckaert
ISBN 978 1 78592 328 9
eISBN 978 1 78450 644 5

PANDAS and PANS in School Settings
A Handbook for Educators
Edited by Patricia Rice Doran
Foreword by Diana Pohlman
ISBN 978 1 84905 744 8
eISBN 978 1 78450 166 2

SOLUTIONS FOCUSED SPECIAL EDUCATION

Practical and Inclusive
Strategies for All Educators

EDITED BY NICK BURNETT

Jessica Kingsley *Publishers*
London and Philadelphia

First published in 2019
by Jessica Kingsley Publishers
73 Collier Street
London N1 9BE, UK
and
400 Market Street, Suite 400
Philadelphia, PA 19106, USA

www.jkp.com

Library of Congress Cataloging in Publication Data
A CIP catalog record for this book is available from the Library of Congress

British Library Cataloguing in Publication Data
A CIP catalogue record for this book is available from the British Library

ISBN 978 1 78592 527 6
eISBN 978 1 78450 916 3

Printed and bound in the United States

This book is dedicated to my wife Sally Burnett for her unswerving support and encouragement to follow my dreams oxox

Contents

Preface

Nick Burnett

This book is not intended to be a detailed review of the issues and challenges facing special education. Nor is it intended to promote a more or less inclusive view of education as a whole, although by adopting a Solutions Focused (SF) approach to special education I would suggest that the system may become more inclusive. Instead it is a reflection of my experience of special education over 30 years in a wide range of countries across the world as a teacher, leader and more recently trainer, coach and consultant.

The motivation for my role in editing and contributing to so many of the chapters came from the intersection of my background in special education, coming into contact with my increasing work in coaching, and more specifically SF approaches. With an increased understanding of what is meant by taking a SF approach, I believe it has a lot to offer those working in both special and mainstream education at all levels.

This book is an attempt to initiate dialogue into how we can reframe special education into more about what individuals can do and achieve, as opposed to what they can't do, at both practitioner and system levels, and in doing so enable education to become more inclusive.

It is not meant in any way to denigrate the many wonderful special educators who support incredible achievements with individuals who have special educational needs and gain great reward from seeing what are often very small improvements (or in some cases the slowing down of degenerative conditions).

Neither is it suggesting that some (many) in special education are not operating in effective ways and they may be operating either deliberately, or otherwise, through a SF approach. Rather, it is intended to build on the work of these innovative practitioners to share where things are working, and to explore where things might be 'even better if…' It is an attempt to begin to reimagine special education in a more solution/strengths/ability focused way at both a system and practitioner level.

The focus of this work is to identify what the tangible benefits are for the students, schools and education systems in moving towards Solutions Focused Special Education (SFSE).

In an online discussion in 2013 on what was already working, it became clear that, not unsurprisingly, there were a number of examples of good practice already in place around many of the areas needed to enable SFSE to be a reality.

To give some structure to enable both exploration of what was already working around the world, and also to assist in developing SFSE thinking and sharing of current practice further, the following themes emerged and there is a chapter on each theme:

- system philosophy and practices for a system that works
- school leadership
- diagnoses or solutions: different pathways for supporting students with diverse learning needs
- human resources
- teaching and learning processes
- behaviour support
- partnerships with family and community.

The authors of each of the chapters was also offered the following framework for their writing of any case studies, although they each cover their subject in their own way.

- background – including the following:
  » who is included in the case study being mindful of confidentiality
  » why this approach was chosen
- more detail on the approach used, identifying how it:
  » is SF for the individual and those supporting the individual

» supports:

    — an individualised approach

    — success

    — raising aspirations

» is based on the premise of best interest for the student

» could lead to tangible benefits for a 'resource-led' system.

The focus of the largely practical nature of the chapters is to provide 'practice-based evidence' to support those wishing to implement SFSE. I often challenge those in education who ask whether something is 'evidence-based practice'. Whilst it is ultimately the aim to implement practices that are, someone has to trial practice in order to gather enough evidence for it to be deemed evidence-based practice.

The book finishes with a conclusion drawing on the key emerging messages from the chapters. It also includes a glimpse into what the future might hold and some current case studies about the emerging use of exponential technologies that are likely to have a profound impact on all of education in the next few years and beyond.

It should be noted that there is a range of styles of writing across the chapters, and this is deliberate in allowing a range of 'voices' to be heard to allow for the emergence of something greater than the book being in just one 'voice'.

Before getting into the chapters, I believe it is important to explore some of the concepts and potential 'elephants in the room' that sit behind SF approaches, even more so in the special education space, and it is to these that I will now turn.

Introduction

THE ELEPHANTS IN THE ROOM!

The purpose of this section of the introduction is to name the 'elephants in the room' which are likely to be influencing the lens through which the reader is accessing, or not, the rest of the book and in doing so bring assumptions and beliefs to the surface.

Whilst there may well be more, I've identified three particular 'elephants' to explore before we get into the main focus of the book, the possible way to adopt a Solutions Focused (SF) approach to special education, which, if done well, will, I believe, lead to a more inclusive education system.

1. Disability: an unnecessary duality

2. Special education versus inclusion

3. Solutions Focused Special Education – a paradox?

In line with adopting a Solutions Focused approach, the aim of naming these 'elephants' is to be aware of the potential biases we all hold around what is right and what is wrong and what might sit behind this. Before exploring the first 'elephant', the philosophical basis of 'where' I am coming from will be briefly explored to enable the reader to assess how they feel about my interpretations.

At the risk of losing some readers by moving into the philosophical realm, I believe unless we have an understanding of 'where' the writer is coming from, it is difficult for us to assess accurately how we feel about their views. Furthermore, in a recent review of the literature into the fields of special education and inclusion, I found a lack of clear statements regarding the writers' philosophical underpinnings in which their writing was situated. In an attempt to rectify this, in relation to this chapter, I will now briefly identify the key elements underpinning critical realism.

Critical realism

This chapter is grounded in a meta-theory known as critical realism developed by Roy Bhaskar (1978, 1989a, 1989b, 1998) and what follows is a very brief introduction to some key tenets. Critical realism is founded on the belief that:

- There is a world existing independently of our knowledge of it and therefore all knowledge is fallible.

- Knowledge is transient and it is important to recognise that it is relative to the historical, social and political context in which it was produced.

- In social reality, individuals both reproduce and transform social structures, as well as form them, whilst social structures both shape and place constraints on individuals, but are also the result of continuous activity by individuals.

- Human actions may be associated with unacknowledged conditions, unintended consequences, the exercise of tacit skills and/or unconscious motivation, and therefore critical realism offers a way forward through its emancipatory/transformational potential.

- Social structures are real things which have causal powers which may, or may not, be activated.

- Research undertaken from a critical realist paradigm attempts to interpret the world in order to bring about change.

I will refer to these key tenets, where appropriate, during the rest of this chapter to support the suggestions put forward.

Elephant Number 1: Disability: an unnecessary duality

The first 'elephant' I'm going to discuss is the issue of disability and the duality that's often positioned between social and medical. The purpose of starting here is that in many countries the access to additional support is based on a diagnosis.

Whilst it is necessary to briefly explore, from a critical realist perspective, the issues around competing paradigms within an under-standing of disability, as this informs the later discussion on special education and inclusion, it is beyond the scope of this section to go into significant depth and analysis on this issue, although a number of other researchers have done so and I would refer you to them as a starting point (Barton, 1987; Low, 2006; Slee, 1998).

Looking at a range of literature into current practice and beliefs about disability, it tends either to argue for the need to identify disability as within the individual so that appropriate interventions can be developed (Kauffman, 1999; Kavale and Mostert, 2005) or to argue for the need to identify disability within societal structures and beliefs which create the disability rather than it being inherently within the individual (Barton, 1987; Oliver, 1986; Soder, 1989).

The individual or, as it is often referred to, medical model of disability believes that all the ensuing difficulties are within the individual and therefore their 'faults' need to be addressed in order to put these right. For many, this is what special education was founded on and it continues to operate from this paradigm (Oliver, 1986; Tomlinson, 1985) with a medical diagnosis being required in a number of countries around the world to access special education services and funding.

For a number of years now, there has been greater acceptance of the social view of disability (Clark *et al.*, 1995; Thomas and Loxley, 2001). This is at odds with the way special education has been and is structured and this will be explored in more detail in the next section.

In relation to the social view of disability, some argue that 'difference is not a euphemism for defect, for abnormality, for a problem to be worked out through technical and assimilationist education policies, diversity is a social fact' (Armstrong, Armstrong and Barton, 1998, p.34). Therefore, it is argued that differences and diversity should be promoted and that we need to fully understand these in order to know what adaptations and changes are required to enable those with impairments to enjoy improved wellbeing and equality of access to educational opportunities.

In line with a critical realist view of causal relations, that there is a dual character to individuals and society, that is, structure and agency, an increasing number of writers are starting to suggest that this duality is unhelpful in reality (Low, 2006; Norwich, 2002; Terzl, 2005). To exemplify this, it could be seen that for those who would argue that the social view of disability is the totality of the interrelationship, the danger could become that if there is an absence of any specification of the concept of difference, how can difference be celebrated, and how can an appropriate educational experience be developed and provided?

Shakespeare, among others, argues that the social model of disability needs to be reconceptualised to include the experience of impairment (Lindsay, 2003; Norwich, 1993; Shakespeare, 1993; Terzl, 2005). Norwich (1993) believes that those who advocate the social model of disability can be contradictory in their arguments when they state that all the difficulty lies within society's inability to adapt itself to the characteristics of the child, whilst also demanding that there should be an interaction between the individual and the school. Indeed, from a critical realist perspective, it is only through the interrelationship between individual and society that transformation will be brought about.

It is therefore proposed that a move away from the duality of views currently present within many of the fields of disability towards an acceptance of the causal relations between society and the individual is helpful in providing a way forward, particularly in the fields of inclusion and special education. Ideas and case studies around how this might be implemented will be explored in a number of the following chapters.

Elephant Number 2: Special education versus inclusion

The issue of inclusion is high on the educational reform agenda in many countries and can be said to be a global phenomenon (Timmons, 2002), with individual countries and regions within countries being at different stages of the journey. Why then are we in a state of stasis or regression in some countries in relation to developing a more inclusive educational system?

What I propose to examine is where we currently are in relation to developing a more inclusive educational system and to briefly de-construct current issues within special education and inclusion, before exploring SFSE as a possible reconstruction leading to a more inclusive education system.

Current position

Inclusion was originally premised on a desire for a radical change to the whole fabric of schooling (Graham and Slee, 2007). Instead of profound change, what is being found is that in many circumstances the word 'inclusion' is being used as a means for ensuring the status quo (Graham and Slee, 2007; Slee, 2001).

One of the difficulties with the move to inclusion, or towards a more inclusive education system, has been a lack of agreed definition of what is meant by inclusion. Alongside this are the often-polarised discourses prevalent in special education versus inclusion. Proponents of inclusion have often taken a very moral stance in terms of why inclusion is *good* and special education is *bad*. In doing so, I believe that they have either alienated some of those who could potentially assist in the move towards a more inclusive education system, or caused those who feel 'threatened' to 'adopt' the word in the name of reinvented special education practice (Slee, 1996).

Through this 'adoption' the word 'inclusion' has almost become unusable in any coherent manner. The word 'inclusion' is now *de rigueur* in all mission statements, policy documents and political speeches and so has become a cliché which is obligatory in the discourse of all right-minded people (Thomas and Loxley, 2001), and thus has become a 'suitcase' word, where the word is used in such a way that people put whatever they want into its meaning. Kauffman (1999) states that he believes the word 'inclusion' has become virtually meaningless, being used as a catchword for a whole range of potentially opposite approaches, citing what Salman Rushdie has called the new incomprehensibility.

Regarding the desire for developing more inclusive educational systems, there are a number of key areas that I believe are worthy of further examination in relation to the current position of special education.

Special education

I have deliberately entitled this section 'Special education versus inclusion' as I think this is at the core of the difficulty in moving from where special education currently is to where I believe it needs to be. If the discussion remains at just the level of criticising the other view then I believe progress will be very slow. In accepting inclusion as a global phenomenon which has been enshrined in a number of international agreements, surely the focus should be on how we make it work in practice?

I am of the opinion that those in special education are well placed to promote the needs of the individual student and work towards more inclusive educational environments. In addition, I also believe that leaders do have the ability to be transformational agents and therefore can and should attempt to make a difference. I noted in my analysis of leadership styles that some Heads/Principals were very proactive in developing more inclusive educational environments and were working to close or change their current schools. This was borne out of the strong belief that inclusion was the way forward (Burnett, 2005).

In contrast, others were doing everything within their power to keep their special school operating as it was, albeit making it more effective (Burnett, 2005). In spite of this, I believe that the majority of leaders in special education are not consciously trying to stop inclusion just to further their own interests. What is happening at a subconscious level is much more difficult to access, although this is seen as a key tenet of critical realism and, through making these beliefs transparent, it offers a way forward.

In line with this critical realist view of knowledge being fallible and transient, MacIntyre, quoted in Scott (2000, p.16), identifies that discourses or 'traditions of thought' are manifested in human behaviour but are subject to change and decay. These discourses are often nested within 'supra-discourses' and these are best defined as the way a society or group of people understand the nature of the world and how it can be known. In other words, their beliefs. These not only influence the type of discourse operating within the group but also the rate of decay of these discourses. Therefore, what is accepted as the 'truth' by society or groups within society is not so much about its level of correctness, but more about its function in how particular communities of people construct and reconstruct forms of knowledge. Thus what is seen as 'real' by those communities at particular times of history could be seen as a form of 'virtual reality' (Giddens, 1984).

Currently, our school systems are weighed down with discourses of deficit and disadvantage manifested in categories used to sort children. Categorised labels 'that have defined the universe of educational exceptionality are formal explanations of educational success and failure that are institutionalised in important ways in the practices that separate the more or less successful students from each other' (Carrier, 1989, p.212). These cultural constructions of difference, school success and failure are represented in personal beliefs, attitudes and values and shape how educators interact with students (Carrington, 2000). We need to carefully consider what beliefs currently inform our construction of 'special' and 'regular' schooling.

In relation to the historical context of special education there are competing views as to why it was established and why it continues in spite of the apparent overwhelming support for the concept of inclusion. Tomlinson (1982) identified that many in special education would see their profession as one premised on the liberal ideology of benevolent humanitarianism: the duty that a society has to care for its weaker members. Many others believe that the continuance of special education is down to an attempt by teachers and administrators in regular schools to maintain the status of the special education 'industry' (Fuchs and Fuchs, 2005; Fulcher, 1989; Slee, 2001). Slee (2001) is particularly self-critical of his time as a special educator for giving him more sophisticated methods and approaches aimed at promulgating special education and he describes himself as a 'card-carrying designator of disability' (p.170).

The expansion of special education has also been linked to professional interests, with a rejection of the suggestion that much of the expansion is down to accident, spontaneous adjustment, progress and benevolence (Tomlinson, 1985). Tomlinson (1985) cites Archer in affirming her belief that educational structures are a result of the interests of those social groups who manage education. In relation to special education, she believes educationalists, psychologists and medical practitioners all have a vested interest in expanding the numbers of pupils identified as 'special'. Those working in special education have an interest in increasing numbers as do mainstream teachers who are under the pressures of greater accountability as well as possibly preferring to place the problem with the child as opposed to their teaching.

Thomas and Loxley (2001) believe the growth and maintenance of special education has been as much about expediency as oppression, with a focus on the psychology of politicians, planners and administrators, stating that to justify their position they need to identify problems and then provide visible solutions to these problems. Just moving the funding into mainstream education to assist it in becoming more inclusive would be seen as an abdication of responsibility as it could not be seen: 'The special system is thereby geared toward providing visible "services" designed to help' (Thomas and Loxley, 2001, p.43).

My view as a former special school headteacher is mixed. I have long held concerns regarding the way education is structured and its outdated basis but I guess like many others I distanced myself from this when working in special education and just focused on doing my best for all students. I do believe that the majority of people I met and worked with in special education would fit into this category. Although I did meet those who appeared to wish to promote self-interests, even in those cases it was often due to a belief that special education was the best option. In addition, professional vulnerability in changing times frequently supports the maintenance of the status quo or superficial changes that don't really get to the root of the underlying problems with current policy and practice in special education.

I would suggest that it was never really discussed in detail and most people are focused on the 'here and now' rather than on the 'what should be'. As Thomas and Loxley say:

> The past hundred years have seen the development of mechanisms, procedures, measuring instruments and practices which have had the object of identifying and moving pupils into segregated forms of schooling. The notion that special education operates as a filtering device to render more manageable the majority of the system has now become part of the received wisdom of critical thinking about special education. (2001, p.76)

Given these difficulties with the current formulation of special education and the polarised views of many involved, is there a possible way forward?

A possible way forward

The issue of special education is inextricably linked to how education as a whole is conceptualised and constructed. The hope is that an inclusive philosophy underpins the reconceptualisation and reconstruction so that education is truly inclusive of all members of society.

Many see inclusion as really about extending the comprehensive ideal in education, and argue that therefore the drive should be more towards what the education system needs to look like in order to promote tolerance, diversity and equity (Ainscow, 1995; Carrington, 1999; Lipsky and Gartner, 2005b; Skrtic, 1991; Slee, 2001; UNESCO, 2000) rather than the current focus on 'special educational needs' and all the difficulties and baggage that this terminology brings (Barton, 1987; Clark *et al.*, 1995).

Theories dealing with democratic community (Dewey, 1916) provide opportunities to rethink how we can improve acceptance of difference and create communities inclusive of all members of society (Turner and Louis, 1996). Separation or stereotyping differences creates divisions and status systems that detract from the democratic nature of the community and the dignity of the individual. Others also argue that education should be guided by democratic principles (Artiles, 2003; Lipsky and Gartner, 2005a; Nilholm, 2006; Skrtic, Sailor and Gee, 1996) rather than any other factors currently in play such as the demands of the marketisation of education (Bines, 1995). As Sultana states:

> ...schooling cannot be divorced from the wider social order, and schools and educators are not and cannot be 'neutral' and 'apolitical' channels for equally 'neutral' and 'apolitical' knowledge. Whatever we make happen in schools – constantly and inevitably – gives messages defining what it means to be 'human', 'good' and 'normal' in particular social contexts. (Sultana, quoted in Barton, 1987, p.54)

The debate needs to focus on the type of society we wish to be part of and the key values that guide this. In line with a critical realist view this may, by necessity, differ in different countries depending on their social, historical and political context. I believe an important role for the international bodies is to give guidance as to what this might mean across the world. But in promoting diversity I believe all need to be careful about trying to impose their views onto others.

Skrtic (1995), along with others, articulates a more radical need to restructure schools rather than just the focus on inclusion (Lipsky and Gartner, 2005a; Slee, 2001). In my view there needs to be some strident discussion at senior levels within communities as to what is the aim and purpose of education and what values guide decisions. In the current absence of much of this debate, certainly at a political level, if it is accepted that making our education system more inclusive is the 'right' thing to do, is it not incumbent on all of us to explore how we can make this more of a reality?

SFSE is put forward as a way of moving forward from the current entrenched positions found in many countries around the world, and how this might be achieved is shared in the subsequent chapters.

Elephant Number 3: SFSE – a paradox?

I believe it is important to examine the apparent paradox of people (students) being constrained by a system that categorises them as 'having special needs' or goes further to make a diagnosis of a disorder, particularly when that might come about by committee agreement that brackets services within the confines of the disorder. From the critical realist perspective of being unconditionally respected, as having agency, being experts in their own life and being resourceful, adopting a SF stance towards them means looking at the position we are taking when we're thinking about supporting them to live the best life they can live in a good-enough world.

This paradox makes for tension – how can we ethically *be* within the SF paradigm in our work with students classified as 'special educational needs (SEN)'? Aren't we forced to move back from the position of writing White Papers about 'SF in SEN' to take in the whole world of education where students wouldn't be classified and diagnosed for reasons that are in the interest of services rather than in the interest of the individual?

It is proposed that in being fully aware of the paradox that is SFSE, we acknowledge but do not accept where we currently are in relation to education, and take an overall long-term view that if the system becomes more SF then the need for separate segregated provision will diminish (or even disappear).

SF approach

There are an increasing number of excellent books for those who wish to dig deeper into the world of SF approaches (please refer to the References section for suggestions). What follows is, I hope, enough information and content to enable the reader to have enough understanding and background to help explain the practical approaches described in the subsequent chapters. I also want to draw attention to the possible question as to whether we should use 'Solution Focused' or 'Solutions Focused'. There are many more knowledgeable SF thought leaders who could articulate what the difference is and whether it is important but where possible I have tried to use 'Solutions Focused' to try and mitigate against the common misunderstanding that when named as 'Solution Focused' it is suggesting there is one solution. This, in my view, is the very antithesis of SF. At its heart SF is 'practice-based evidence' with the generation of numerous options as opposed to the 'right answer' and there will be more on this shortly. But in short, whether authors have named it as Solutions Focused or Solution Focused, we are all coming from the same premise.

SF approaches originate from Solution Focused Brief Therapy developed by Steve de Shazer and Insoo Kim Berg in America in the 1970s and de Shazer's work has made a great impact in the world of therapeutic change over the past 40 years. Subsequently their ideas have spread, resulting in SF practice in many contexts, including social work, child protection, education, and group work, amongst others.

The SF approach values simplicity in philosophy and language and aims to discover 'what works' in a given situation, simply and practically. The focus on solutions (not problems), the future (not the past) and on what's going well (rather than what's gone wrong) leads to a positive and pragmatic way to work with organisations and individuals.

The major paradigm shift is from a problem focus to a solutions focus.

One definition of SF is: 'Change is happening all the time... The simple way to change is to find useful change and amplify it' (Jackson and McKergow, 2007, p.xvii).

When something's wrong, we have the idea that the way to change is to find what's wrong and fix it. The usual strategy goes something like this:

1. Diagnose the problem.

2. Discover the cause and address weaknesses.

3. Make and implement detailed action plans.

This strategy works well for situations where things are fixed and well known in advance, and where your efforts don't change the situation dramatically.

Once you introduce people into the equation, however, things become more complicated. For decades psychologists have been trying to find ways to classify people and their problems so that the basic 'problem-focused' strategy will work. Whilst this remains, for many, the dominant paradigm, the results are often far less than the promotional material would have you believe.

SF takes a quite different approach to working out what to do. To start with, it doesn't use any of the conventional problem-focused steps above. This is a significant shift in the worldview for many. People often ask: how can you make progress without knowing exactly what the problem is? The 50 years of experience, development, research and practice into the SF approach shows differently.

SF has three contrasting steps to the problem-focused approach above:

1. Describe what's wanted instead.

2. Discover what's working already and find strengths.

3. Take small steps.

The reasons for this approach become clearer when we have a look at the contrast between working with a problem focus and a solutions focus.

Table 0.1: What's the focus?

Problem Focus	Solution Focus
What's wrong	What's wanted
What needs fixing	What's working
Blame	Progress
Control	Influence
Causes in the past	'Counters' in the past
The expert knows best	Collaboration
Deficits & weaknesses	Resources & strengths
Complications	Simplicity
	Actions

Source: Jackson and McKergow (2007)

At the highest level, there are three key principles for working in a Solutions Focused way:

1. If it ain't broke, don't fix it.

   By 'broke', we mean that somebody in the organisation is dissatisfied and wants something to be different. We start to work with the people who want something different and are prepared to do something about it – not the others (who may be ambivalent or who do not see any need for improvement).

2. Once you know what works, do more of it.

   If you note when the solution is happening already, whether spontaneously, by accident, or even only in part, you have priceless knowledge.

3. If it's not working, do something different.

   Although we usually make progress by using the second of these principles, just occasionally something else is required.

It sounds simple and it is, but simple is not the same as easy, and it is surprising the lure that problem talk holds – for those who want differences in their lives and organisations, and for those whose job it is to help them.

To help guide the overall SF approach within SFSE we will be drawing on the relevant 'Clues', as originally devised by the Association for the Quality Development of Solution Focused Consultancy and Training and now taken on by Solution Focus in Organisations (SFiO), for granting full membership when submitting a project:

- Change is happening all the time – our role is to find useful change and amplify it.

- Resource orientation rather than deficit orientation.

- A 'not knowing' stance of having as few assumptions about the client as possible.

- Deeming clients to be the expert on their own lives and desires.

- A respectful, non-blaming and co-operative stance.

- An interactional view (in between not 'inside' a person).

- Working towards their client's goals from within their client's frames of reference, while keeping their own (external) perspective.

- Treating each case as different and developing the process according to what the client says rather than imposing a fit into a theoretical or conceptual framework – 'the process emerges differently each time based on what the clients say/do/want'.

As this is such a different worldview from the dominant 'problem-focused' paradigm in which most people and certainly nearly all systems operate, it's worth unpacking the 'Clues' further to help readers make sense of what follows in this book.

Change is happening all the time – our role is to find useful change and amplify it

If you stop to consider what was 'true' yesterday then it might well be that something has changed to challenge that assumption, particularly when we consider this in relation to human beings. I have a hypothesis that when most people say they don't like change it's because they remember the 'bad' bits around change as opposed to any useful bits. The SF approach is to become an expert in identifying any useful elements and then to draw attention to them through questioning and reflecting.

Resource orientation rather than deficit orientation

SF approaches look to explore what people have as opposed to what they don't have. A common SF tool is called scaling where people are asked something like: 'On a scale of 1–10 where 1 is the worst things can be and 10 is the best things can be, where are you currently at in relation to...' Let's say they answer '4', the follow-up question would be: 'So what gets it that high?' So the focus is on what the person has to get them to 4 as opposed to what they haven't got, that is, the gap between 4 and 10. Deceptively simple but incredibly powerful when used appropriately, this is often followed with: 'What could you do to move one point up the scale?' Therefore, adding that improvement is gradual and uses the power of small steps.

A 'not knowing' stance of having as few assumptions about the client as possible

This is linked to the final 'clue', namely that every case is different. We enter most interactions with pre-determined views on the person/situation, and what is possible/not possible. The SF approach is focused on staying curious about what might emerge and staying out of judgement. This is a challenge because as humans we are hardwired and therefore generally very quick to make judgements, positive or negative, about people or situations.

The benefit of this approach is that often much more emerges than we expect.

Deeming clients to be the expert on their own lives and desires

This is a significant one, particularly in education, where we often defer to experts to tell us what to do. Linked to this we might well, consciously or sub-consciously, see ourselves as the expert in a particular area. Whilst we may well bring knowledge and expertise to the conversation, trying to hold off on giving advice as much as possible is key to adopting a SFSE approach. It must also be recognised that there are potentially some challenges to this when working with students with significant difficulties; exploring ways to access their expertise is an important challenge that must be taken on.

A respectful, non-blaming and co-operative stance

I hope and believe that the vast majority of interactions between staff, students and parents are respectful, non-blaming and co-operative. However, it must be recognised that there are times when all of us can shift particularly to 'blaming' if we are not mindful in our interactions and thinking. A key element to the SF approach is staying out of judgement. Whilst this is easy to say, implementing it is harder because, as just mentioned, as human beings we are hardwired to make judgements. There are individual ways of trying to minimise this, and in my case I try to stay in a 'being curious' mindset when someone does or says something I may not agree with. A 'being curious' mindset for me is to wonder what I'm missing or what the other person is experiencing that creates the mismatch. The end point is that we may still not agree but ensuring I am respectful in my responses and searching for what we have in common that encourages a co-operative stance is key to staying in a SF approach.

An interactional view (in between not 'inside' a person)

'The actions in the interaction' is a key frame of thinking in the SF approach, or, put another way, 'It's what happens between the noses not the ears'. What happens in the world happens on the outside. We then see, hear, feel, smell and taste these experiences. All the amazing simultaneous experiences in our minds, what we think, feel, sense, can only get into the shared world experience, actions, by interaction with others. If we want the world to treat us differently then we need to treat the world differently. So the SF maxim is around changing the doing and changing the viewing, rather than merely changing the thinking. From this perspective, the doing gets amplified and comes back to us from a different world.

Working towards their client's goals from within their client's frames of reference, while keeping their own (external) perspective

We need to ensure we are working towards what the students and their family want, wherever possible, whilst remaining impartial enough so that we do not become too engrossed in their desires and can be a potential 'voice of reason' on occasion, drawing on knowledge and experiences that may prove useful to consider. Compassion, as opposed to empathy, is a key component here, in my view, where compassion is a step removed from the experiences (frames of reference). The rationale for this is to try and ensure we do not get too embroiled in what can be very complex lives, and in doing so lose a degree of impartiality that can add value to our interactions with the students and their families.

Treating each case as different and developing the process according to what the client says rather than imposing a fit into a theoretical or conceptual framework – 'the process emerges differently each time based on what the clients say/do/want'

This is a key tenet for me in that we need to be very mindful that we are using our expertise in ways that can suggest possible ways forward as opposed to 'diagnosing' what needs to be done. For example, every person with Autistic Spectrum Disorder I worked with was different. Sure, there appeared to be some similarities with how they experienced the world and approaches that could help them access the learning and development we were offering them. However, they all benefitted from an individualised approach to implementing strategies that might be helpful, as opposed to the rigid implementation of a framework.

Special education – the challenge in being special

It is recognised that who is identified as having or requiring access to special education, within mainstream and specialist provision, varies within countries, never mind across countries. In spite of this there are some commonalities in relation to the way special education is framed within the range of countries I have visited and worked in.

The focus of this book is on those students who have been identified as needing additional supports, either through segregated provision or through additional support in mainstream settings.

Currently, whether placed in mainstream or separate provision, I would suggest that special education is basically a deficit model – what is wrong with the individual – what is special. There are a number of reasons for this:

- It identifies the problem as lying within the individual as opposed to the system, thereby the system does not need to change – I would see this as the major 'broken' bit of special education in relation to one of the key principles of SF: 'If it ain't broke, don't fix it'.

- It provides a method to allocate scarce resources – the greater the need, the more money that goes to the individual (in principle anyway).

Whilst identifying a disability and/or designated learning difficulty may give some clues to initial approaches, in my experience these generally present differently depending on the individual. I propose that viewing individuals, those with special educational needs in this instance, in terms of what they can do and identifying what they have achieved is much more rewarding and beneficial for all. One of the major issues at a system level is how to allocate funds to support individuals and this has driven the need to identify 'labels', so, theoretically at least, those with greater special educational needs access greater funding. Therefore, the system encourages (demands) the use of assessment approaches that label.

Viewing special education through a SF lens

As was discussed in the section exploring the background and rationale to the SF approach, the SF approach is characterised by a drive for simplicity but in an unusual way. In the normal run of things, people attempt to simplify complicated situations by trying to find the 'essence' or defining aspect. One might then expect to use this to find a way forwards, perhaps by finding other similar situations with the same 'essence'. Often the essence of the situation is seen in the 'problem', the thing that we are trying to get away from. SF is not like this at all.

Rather than simplifying by looking for commonalities with other cases, each case is simplified on its own and overlooking aspects which are not contributing to existing performance. These could well be different each time and are developed in conversation with the people involved.

Why view special education through a SF lens?

One of the major reasons to view special education through a SF lens is that, in my view, excellent special education already has many of the key SF assumptions and principles already in place, albeit often not explicitly.

Additionally, there have been ongoing discussions (arguments) in relation to inclusion and the role (or not) of special education for more than 20 years. I would suggest that now is a time to examine a different approach, particularly with the growing demand for significant changes in education as a whole. Whilst not every individual placed within special education may have 'significant' problems, whatever that means, I would argue that special education as a practice could be greatly enhanced by exploring it through a SF lens, and that this 'different' approach to viewing 'special' is worth exploring at both system and practitioner levels.

The emphasis on 'solutions' afforded by the SF lens often leads to a significant shift in mindsets for people being supported and those supporting them. I would suggest the approach becomes even more person centred when working with a strength-based abilities model as opposed to a problem or deficit model on which special education is currently based.

It is useful to identify that there are a number of critical assumptions underpinning the adoption of a SF approach in relation to education and these are drawn from the work of de Shazer, Dolan and Korman (2007), and Furman (2006). These are:

- The pupil is the expert on not only his or her own problems but also the solutions for the problems.

- No problem is always present; there are always exceptions where the problem is not observable.

- Competencies rather than problems should be sought in a strength-oriented approach.

- Children's problems can be redefined as skills to be learned.

- Conditions under which the pupil is successful should be central.

- A major objective is to build on the strengths of the context.

- SF language should be used as much as possible.

- Students are the architects of their own goals and destinies, which means that they should not be tied to diagnostic labels, social backgrounds or personal life histories.

These will be used as a frame of reference for exploring what emerges in a number of the following chapters.

I will now build on and refine these to explore what the key elements of SFSE are.

Key elements to SFSE

- Special education is SF for individuals being supported and those supporting them.

  This draws on a number of the critical assumptions from the previous list, including ensuring that language is Solutions Focused, that is, focused on what is wanted rather than on what is to be avoided. A key frame is that it is Solutions Focused not solutions forced. At times it can be useful for both those being supported and those supporting them to acknowledge the challenges they are facing as a baseline to talk about what is wanted.

- The system supports individuality, success and raises aspirations.

  A major premise of SFSE is that it is a highly individualised approach as distinct from using 'labels' to decide how best to support students. In addition, it is about helping to increase aspirations for all involved and identifying what success is.

- Focus is on an individual's abilities and strengths not disabilities or weaknesses.

  Discussion and focus is on what abilities and strengths the individual brings to any situation that might be helpful and useful in moving towards success and achievement.

- It is premised on the 'best interests' of the individual.

The focus of interventions is on the best interests of the individual as opposed to the best interests of the system, school, teachers or parents. Although it is anticipated that this is generally the case already, ensuring this is the explicit focus ensures the attention remains at the individual level.

- There are tangible benefits for a 'resource-led' system.

Whilst this might potentially seem at odds with the previous key element, the current structure is still highly systemised and for SFSE to have impact and success the system does need to be able to identify tangible resource benefits alongside individual benefits.

References

Ainscow, M. (1995) 'Special needs through school improvement: school improvement through special needs.' In C. Clark, A. Dyson and A. Millward (eds) *Towards Inclusive Schools?* London: David Fulton.

Armstrong, F., Armstrong, F. and Barton, L. (1998) 'From theory to practice: special education and the social relations of academic production.' In C. Clark, A. Dyson and A. Millward (eds) *Theorising Special Education*. London: Routledge.

Artiles, A.J. (2003) 'Special education's changing identity: paradoxes and dilemmas in views of culture and space.' *Harvard Educational Review*, 73(2), 164–202.

Barton, L. (ed.) (1987) *The Politics of Special Educational Needs*. Lewes: Falmer Press.

Bhaskar, R. (1978) *A Realist Theory of Science* (Second edition). London: Verso.

Bhaskar, R. (1989a) *The Possibility of Naturalism* (Second edition). Hemel Hempstead: Harvester.

Bhaskar, R. (1989b) *Reclaiming Reality: A Critical Introduction to Contemporary Philosophy*. London: Verso.

Bhaskar, R. (1998) 'Societies.' In M. Archer, R. Bhaskar, A. Collier, T. Lawson and A. Norrie (eds) *Critical Realism: Essential Readings*. London: Routledge.

Bines, H. (1995) 'Special educational needs in the market place.' *Journal of Education Policy*, 10(2), 157–171.

Burnett, N. (2005) *Leadership and SEN: Meeting the Challenge in Special and Mainstream Settings*. London: David Fulton.

Carrier, J. (1989) 'Sociological perspectives on special education.' *New Education*, 11, 21–31.

Carrington, S. (1999) 'Inclusion needs a different school culture.' *International Journal of Inclusive Education*, 3(3), 257–268.

Carrington, S. (2000) 'Accommodating the needs of diverse learners: teacher beliefs.' Unpublished doctoral thesis, University of Queensland, St. Lucia, Brisbane.

Clark, C., Dyson, A., Millward, A. and Skidmore, D. (1995) 'Dialectical analysis, special needs and schools as organisations.' In C. Clark, A. Dyson, A. Millward and D. Skidmore (eds) *Towards Inclusive Schools?* London: David Fulton.

de Shazer, S. and Berg, I.K. (1995) 'The Brief Therapy Tradition', in *Propagations: Thirty Years of Influence from the Mental Research Institute* (edited by John Weakland and Wendel Ray). New York: Haworth Press.

de Shazer, S., Dolan, Y.M. and Korman, H. (2007) *More Than Miracles: The State of the Art of Solution Focused Brief Therapy.* New York: Haworth Press.

Dewey, J. (1916) *Democracy and Education.* New York: Macmillan.

Fuchs, D. and Fuchs, L.S. (2005) 'Inclusive schools movement and the radicalization of special education reform.' In D. Mitchell (ed.) *Special Educational Needs and Inclusive Education: Major Themes in Education. Volume II: Inclusive Education.* London: Routledge Falmer.

Fulcher, G. (1989) *Disabling Policies? A Comparative Approach to Education Policy and Disability.* Lewes: Falmer Press.

Furman, B. (2006) Kids' skills, playful and practical solution-finding with children (video). Available at www.kidsskills.org (accessed 2/10/2018).

Giddens, A. (1984) *The Constitution of Society.* Cambridge: Polity Press.

Graham, L.J., and Slee, R. (2007) An Illusory Interiority: Interrogating the discourse/s of inclusion [Electronic Version]. *Educational Philosophy and Theory*, Online Early Articles, 1–17. Available at https://eprints.qut.edu.au/57604 (accessed 20/10/2018).

Jackson, P.Z., and McKergow, M. (2007) *The Solutions Focus* (Second edition). London: Nicholas Brearley Publishing.

Kauffman, J.M. (1999) 'Commentary: Today's special education and its messages for tomorrow.' *The Journal of Special Education*, 32(4), 244–254.

Kavale, K.A., and Mostert, M.P. (2005) 'Rivers of ideology, islands of evidence.' In D. Mitchell (ed.) *Special Educational Needs and Inclusive Education: Major Themes in Education. Volume II: Inclusive Education.* London: Routledge Falmer.

Lindsay, G. (2003) 'Inclusive education: a critical perspective.' *British Journal of Special Education*, 30(1), 3–12.

Lipsky, D.K., and Gartner, A. (2005a) 'Inclusive education: a requirement of a democratic society.' In D. Mitchell (ed.) *Special Educational Needs and Inclusive Education: Major Themes in Education. Volume II: Inclusive Education.* London: Routledge Falmer.

Lipsky, D.K., and Gartner, A. (2005b) 'Equity requires inclusion: the future for all students with disabilities.' In D. Mitchell (ed.) *Special Educational Needs and Inclusive Education: Major Themes in Education. Volume II: Inclusive Education.* London: Routledge Falmer.

Low, C. (2006) 'Some ideologies of disability.' *Journal of Research in Special Educational Needs*, 6(2), 108–111.

Nilholm, C. (2006) 'Special education, inclusion and democracy.' *European Journal of Special Needs Education*, 21(4), 431–445.

Norwich, B. (1993) 'Has "special educational needs" outlived its usefulness?' In J. Visser and G. Upton (eds) *Special Education in Britain after Warnock.* London: Fulton.

Norwich, B. (2002) 'Education, inclusion and individual differences: recognising and resolving dilemmas.' *British Journal of Educational Studies*, 50(4), 482–501.

Oliver, M. (1986) 'Social policy and disability: some theoretical issues.' *Disability Handicap and Society*, 1(1), 5–18.

Scott, D. (2000) *Realism and Educational Research: New Perspectives and Possibilities.* London: Routledge Falmer.

Shakespeare, T. (1993) 'Disabled people's self organisation: a new social movement?' *Disability Handicap and Society*, 8(3), 249–264.

Skrtic, T.M. (1991) 'The special education paradox: equity as the way to excellence.' *Harvard Educational Review*, 61(2), 148–206.

Skrtic (1995) *Disability and Democracy: Reconstructing (Special) Education for Postmodernity.* New York: Teachers College Press.

Skrtic, T.M., Sailor, W., and Gee, K. (1996) 'Voice, collaboration and inclusion.' *Remedial and Special Education*, 17(3), 142–157.

Slee, R. (1996) 'Clauses of conditionality: The "reasonable" accommodation of language.' In L. Barton (ed.) *Disability and Society: Emerging Issues and Insights*. London: Longman.

Slee, R. (1998) 'The politics of theorising special education.' In C. Clark, A. Dyson and A. Millward (eds) *Theorising Special Education*. London: Routledge.

Slee, R. (2001) 'Social justice and the changing directions in educational research: the case of inclusive education.' *International Journal of Inclusive Education*, 5(2/3), 167–177.

Soder, M. (1989) 'Disability as a social construct: the labelling approach revisited.' *European Journal of Special Needs Education*, 4(2), 117–129.

Terzl, L. (2005) 'Beyond the dilemma of difference: the capability approach to disability and special educational needs.' *Journal of Philosophy in Education*, 39(3), 443–459.

Thomas, G. and Loxley, A. (2001) *Deconstructing Special Education and Constructing Inclusion*. Buckingham: Open University Press.

Timmons, V. (2002) 'International perspectives on inclusion: some concluding thoughts'. *Exceptionality Education Canada*, 12, 187–192.

Tomlinson, S. (1982) *A Sociology of Special Education*. London: Routledge and Kegan Paul.

Tomlinson, S. (1985) 'The expansion of special education.' *Oxford Review of Education*, 11(2), 157–165.

Turner, C.S.V. and Louis, K.S. (1996) 'Society's response to differences: a sociological perspective.' *Remedial and Special Education*, 17(3), 134–141. First Published 1 May 1996. https://doi.org/10.1177/074193259601700303.

UNESCO (2000) *Dakar Framework for Action: Education for All: Meeting Our Collective Commitments*. Paris: UNESCO.

Chapter 1

SOLUTIONS FOCUSED SPECIAL EDUCATION SYSTEM PHILOSOPHY AND PRACTICES FOR A SYSTEM THAT WORKS

Dr Geoffrey James, Professor Andrew Turnell,
Professor Eileen Munro and Terry Murphy

Introduction
Nick Burnett

What follows are two areas of thoughts, ideas and practices that could help identify some clues as to how SFSE could be implemented at a system level. The first section is written by Dr Geoffrey James and reflects his view on the current Solutions Focused (SF) landscape in UK schools, and the second section draws on the significant systems work developed and implemented across a range of systems by Professor Andrew Turnell, Professor Eileen Munro and Terry Murphy in the child protection field; this is the Signs of Safety approach. Whilst these are obviously in different fields, both Andrew and I feel that the special education field is so connected to the child protection field (in both its broadest and narrowest senses), that this is therefore a really good fit to explore possibilities.

Given that there are a number of authors in what is probably one of the more complex chapters to unpack, it is separated by both section and preferred author's style, starting with Dr Geoffrey James' work in schools.

A view of the SF landscape in UK schools
Dr Geoffrey James

The overall focus of this book is to identify the benefits for the students, schools and education systems in moving towards SFSE. These three contexts in which SF practice and its practice-informed theory can make a positive difference are entangled with one another, mutually interacting.

The specific focus of my section in this chapter is the movement of students, schools and education systems towards SF Education (SFE) in general and towards a particular aspect of SF Special Education (SFSE), but I will first start with an exploration of some of the assumptions that sit behind the current education system.

Notes on problem solving

> *When you have eliminated the impossible whatever remains, however improbable, must be the truth.*

(Sherlock Holmes)

When we come up against problems that crop up for individuals, for groups of people or for an organisation, we usually focus on the problem itself, isolating it and subjecting it to a detailed analysis, to strip it down by the process of elimination until we can see what caused it.

This is based on a simple assumption, so widespread that it seems no less than common sense; the problem contains the solution. If you take the problem apart carefully, the solution will be revealed like a pearl in an oyster. Following Holmes' admonition, the problem exists only until we find the solution, at which point it collapses and the problem is solved. Further than that, if a problem does not have a solution, it ceases to be a problem and becomes just another fact of life.

Suppose that for all our dogged persistence we fail to solve the problem. Sherlock Holmes himself gave up on cases, when the link between cause and effect eluded him. The complexity of the problem can obscure the cause–effect relationship to such an extent that the elimination of the impossible becomes impossible. So why did Arthur Conan Doyle give his fictional sleuth impossible cases? Maybe he wanted to point out that even Holmes, with his IQ of 190, could sometimes be stumped by this awful truth: that the solution may not lie within the problem.

Why explanation is important

The SF approach has an obstacle in its way into the educational system. Existing practices, which foreground the top-down control of children and their learning by adults, have clear and simple structures. Rote learning in class, and reward and punishment inside and outside the classroom, are so well established as to be largely unchallenged. This is despite a long-standing critique of the effects of reward and punishment on children and staff in schools, which often operate in a directly opposite way to what is intended (Kohn, 1999). Why, in the face of evidence, are these methods so persistent? In my view, one reason is that kinder methods can be written off as being no more than a cosy acceptance of non-compliance and bad behaviour, with no scaffolding of theory and structure to present a real alternative to what is, by what might be instead.

Those of us who make up the SF community understand what Steve de Shazar meant when he said that SF practice does not have a theory. Those new to SF may take it to mean that SF exists as practice without foundations. This is far from the case but in my experience disables SF practice as it attempts to take its place in structures systems.

There is movement in SF development to present practice-informed theory, for example by myself in my 2016 book *Transforming Behaviour in the Classroom: A Solution Focused Guide for New Teachers* and in the work of HESIAN at the University of Hertfordshire (Hertfordshire Enactive Solution focused Interactional and Narrative).[1]

The problem with problems

In Sherlock Holmes' world, the solution of a case lay in pinning down the truth of what caused what, by the process of deduction. 'Elementary, my dear Watson.' There were no grey areas. Holmes could be seen as the ultimate investigative scientist and if he could not solve a problem it proved that science itself could not do more.

But is this all there is to science, a top-down approach, working from the surface of a problem down to its roots? This means making a guess as to what pattern or result we expect to see, collecting evidence from the field and then deducing from general ideas to a specific truth

---

1   For information on HESIAN (Hertfordshire Enactive Solution focused Interactional and Narrative), see www.herts.ac.uk/research/centres-and-groups/philosophy/philosophy-research-activities/hesian.

by testing the hypothesis against observations, from the general to the specific. However, the process of proposing an hypothesis and then using it as a guide for investigation is not the only possible form of science, the only way of understanding nature. More generally, complex systems are regulated by continuous feedback, the control of performance by the consequence of the act performed. In hypothetico-deductive science inferences are the output that powers feedback. If inferences are correct the hypothesis is confirmed, but if they are incorrect the hypothesis must be altered. From this perspective, scientific behavior can be classified both under cybernetics and logic (Medawar, 2008).

In other words, what has come to dominate problem solving is simply one way to go about understanding information processing and control, with its characteristics of information feedback and storage. Cybernetics is defined as the science of control and communication in animals, men and machines. Cybernetic models are usually distinguished by being hierarchical, adaptive and making permanent use of feedback loops. Cybernetics extracts, from whatever context, that which is concerned with information processing and control. It lays special emphasis on the dynamic nature of the system being organised.

This view invites us to make a different kind of exploration which is scientific without being hypothetico-deductive, and which is aimed at arriving at multiple possibilities rather than a single truth. It also moves the discussion of method from the late Victorian era to today. It replaces a model of the brain as a simple, sequential, reactive, stimulus-response mechanism similar to a laptop computer, to a complex, parallel-processing, predictive, dynamic and embodied thing. It also shifts our thinking about consciousness, directing our story to placing consciousness as a by-product of our personal narrative.

This possibility is at a leading edge of neuroscientific thinking. As David Oakley and Peter W. Halligan put it in their article, 'Chasing the Rainbow: The Non-conscious Nature of Being':

> In our view, psychological processing and psychological products are not under the control of consciousness. In particular, we argue that all 'contents of consciousness' are generated by and within non-conscious brain systems in the form of a continuous self-referential personal narrative that is not directed or influenced in any way by the 'experience of consciousness.' This continuously updated personal narrative arises from selective 'internal broadcasting' of outputs from non-conscious

executive systems that have access to all forms of cognitive processing, sensory information, and motor control. The personal narrative provides information for storage in autobiographical memory and is underpinned by constructs of self and agency, also created in non-conscious systems. The experience of consciousness is a passive accompaniment to the non-conscious processes of internal broadcasting and the creation of the personal narrative. In this sense, personal awareness is analogous to the rainbow which accompanies physical processes in the atmosphere but exerts no influence over them. (2017, p.34)

Complex problems

When a complicated problem crops up in something made up of parts, the whole can be disassembled to detect and identify a faulty component, correct or replace it and rebuild the machine back to perfect operation. This is a good strategy where problems are caused by faults in physical systems. To solve this kind of problem we need two things: an expert in the type of system that has developed the fault, someone who can think like a clock or a gas turbine, a software program or a broken collar bone; and a set of the best tools available for the expert to use in fixing it.

It is worth the considerable personal effort on the part of the expert to become an expert, and the financial investment made to provide the suite of tools the expert needs to do the job, because complicated problems are best solved this way.

But what can we do to solve a problem not constructed from physical parts? Imagine a structure where some of the parts and their connections are unknowable to an outside expert, existing only in the mind of the problem-holder, as aspects of their non-conscious personal narrative (Oakley and Halligan, 2017), connecting thought and action, or linking social communication, empathy and doing as you are told. When a person offers this kind of problem as the subject of our work together, who is the expert?

I call this a complex problem to distinguish it from a complicated problem (James 2016), understood with reference to a scientific model, which replaces the cause–effect binary of the hypothetico-deductive empirical model with a layered reality. This model addresses the empiricist claim that the investigator can get full access to the measurable cause of an observable phenomenon, that only what is measurable is real and what is unmeasurable is outside the scope of scientific inquiry.

The critical realist model (Danermark *et al.*, 2002) proposes a deep unobservable level where the non-physical mechanisms exist, the real level; the actual level above this where these mechanisms come into effect; and the empirical level where we can observe the effects. Complexity is tied to the involvement of consciousness and their personal narrative in people's meeting and overcoming human problems. The mantle of the expert is passed from the empiricist doctor/therapist/counsellor/teacher/coach to the client, with the SF therapist/teacher/coach in an enabling role.

What I will now go on to explore is what this might mean in relation to education and the implementation of SFSE.

Working with children and responding to their social, emotional and academic needs in schools raises fundamental questions about practice and the values that underpin practice in education. Schools are set up as places where children are intended to share in opportunities to learn all kinds of things that support their growth and development, in ways that suit them best. Every school is a unique community with its own identity and both mainstream and special schools have their own forms of best practice. Given this, all types of schools share common headline values, one of which is including the child-centred perspective on teaching and learning, listening to and respecting the child's voice. However, there is one corner of the school community where this perspective may go missing.

The origins of some of the practices that are intended to provide opportunities for learning have been around for so long, they have become part of the furniture and insulated from critical analysis by their habitual availability as tools of the trade. One of these is the way schools go about getting children to learn community rules and to follow them, and what they do when children make errors in behaviour, find engagement hard and underachieve or disrupt the planned activity of classrooms. In the current climate where performance is held up to be a goal in itself, if children fail to reach external standards, how does a practice which is centred on the child as a growing and developing individual, rather than as a standard unit of performance, fit in?

Solutions Focused practice, in my case Solutions Focused Coaching in schools, is a case in point and our subject for attention here.

- What works in bringing SF practice into an established system?

- What values underpin inclusive SF practice that match a school's own values?

- Are children to be 'done to' or 'worked with' in school when they come up against barriers to inclusion and learning which may be evidenced by their disengagement and loss of attachment to school?

- And growing from this question; how do the adults in the system, from the teacher and teaching assistant in class, through school managers to the controllers of the levers of power, build SF practice into the work of schools?

In order for SF practice to emerge in face-to-face human interactions, it has to become embedded within educational systems as something that is routinely understood, accepted and brought into action.

How does SF practice become embedded within the educational system?

Solution Focused Brief Therapy (SFBT) emerged 50 years ago in the US and since then has been gradually gaining its place internationally in supporting people confronted with complex issues, at first as a talking therapy in clinical practice and subsequently moving into many other-than clinical fields. In medicine, care planning, business, counselling and coaching work SF practice is welcomed as bringing a fast-acting, non-diagnostic, hopeful and engaging perspective on change.

However, in my experience in the UK, in the field of education it has been a different story and there is a continuing struggle for SF practice to find its place in schools and in the educational system overall. Over more than 20 years working with children struggling with the complexity of schooling, I have demonstrated the relative and specific effectiveness of SF Coaching provided by school staff and/or by an outside SF coach like myself, supporting children's engagement, achievement and inclusion. Individual professionals and schools have taken up the practice wholeheartedly to the clear benefit of students and continue to do so and I share examples of these in Chapter 6 (on the SFSE approach to supporting behaviour). But the education system as a whole, including mainstream and special schools, has not incorporated SF education as routine practice as yet. My personal project over the last 20 years is to increase the capacity of school staff to provide effective preventative support, before schools feel they need to make an outside referral.

Why is the idea of increasing the internal capacity of schools themselves, to meet the needs of children who struggle in school, considered a good one? Because there are 1.3 million staff in UK schools and if only a tiny proportion were to provide SF Coaching, there would be a dramatic shift in both demand for outside specialists like Child and Adolescent Mental Health Services to intervene, and in the effectiveness of schools to meet the diverse pastoral needs of children in all types of schools. At the local level I have been successful, but wider progress is slow and now is the time to make a difference at the systems level.

It is a routine fact that in many areas of life, the solving of complex problems involving people has been handed over from the person experiencing the problem to an outside expert. The strengths, experience and skills needed to arrive at a workable solution are regularly seen as attributes of the external expert, the medical professional, psychologist or teacher. Systems have been constructed to place the expert professional in front of the deficit-defined patient/client via assessment and diagnosis. In some fields there is a realisation that in doing this, a valuable asset is in danger of being overlooked, namely the expertise and experience that the patient/client brings to the meeting. Examples of this are the Positive Health Initiative in the US, supported by a $2.8 million grant from the Robert Wood Johnson Foundation and the positive psychologist Martin Seligman, which positions health and wellbeing as being more than the absence of disease, and the SF Signs of Safety approach to risk and safety in care planning created by Professor Andrew Turnell, Professor Eileen Munro and Terry Murphy, of which more is shared by Andrew later in this chapter.

This paradigm leap is at the heart of SF practice and its practice-informed theory. For those of us who get the idea and have made the shift, changing the focus away from deficits and past failures and towards strengths, resources and success is uncontroversial. But to others, the investment that individuals have made in gaining and exercising expertise, and institutional inertia, are barriers to change.

Since early 2016 I have been working closely with Lincolnshire County Council (LCC) to address the problem of school exclusion. This is a major and growing problem in the UK, with costs to children due to their loss of full-time high-quality education and the threat to their mental and physical health caused by exclusion.

Recorded exclusion rates in the UK have risen annually since 2012. Nearly 7000 children will be permanently excluded this year and 167,000 children are caught up in 330,000 temporary exclusions from school (Department for Education, 2018). Twenty-five thousand of these are primary school aged children, which is the steepest proportional rise. In addition, the National Children's Bureau reports 49,187 children missing from education in 2016–17, with many being illegally off-rolled. Alternative provision is tasked with educating children after expulsion but is overwhelmed by the demand and short of highly qualified staff. Many children are receiving no education while waiting for a place to become available.

This is at an estimated cost of £2.1 billion for each cohort of excluded children. Leading up to 2015, LCC was recorded as a high excluding county. Official guidance from the government and its adviser on behaviour claim that there is no alternative to the 'pipeline' of punishment as a last resort, and without strict discipline and the option of exclusion, schools would descend into chaos. There is no evidence to support the claim. Rather, many schools operate happily and successfully without practising harsh discipline and coercive measures against children who make mistakes. My work, in company with many others using the SF approach in individual schools, demonstrates the claim to be without basis, where schools have adopted child-centred means of guidance and support such as SF Coaching. The distinctive offer that the SF approach makes is to provide a structured way of doing this work.

When I started working with LCC in 2016, SF practice was unknown to the authority as a service approach. I made a connection with the County Inclusion Officer, Mary Meredith, who had written a new strategy, based on the SF approach and challenging the established order. In doing so, the County Council were making a clear policy statement.

To place SF Coaching in context as a broadly based approach, I pointed out that Signs of Safety, already in use in LCC, the NSPCC and regional universities training new teachers, were all promoting the SF approach, and it was widely in use nationally and internationally. Here was an opportunity to bring in an educational way of working which had the capacity to support children in complex and sometimes stressful situations, not a reactive intervention in response to diagnosis, but a way for school staff to act in a timely way to prevent further distress and the risk of damage to a child's life chances.

In 2015/16, one in fifty children in the general population was recognised as having a social, emotional and mental health need (SEMH) (DfE 2017e). In schools for excluded pupils this rose to one in two. Yet the incidence of mental ill health among excluded pupils is likely to be much higher than these figures suggest. Only half of children with clinically diagnosed conduct disorders and a third of children with similarly diagnosed emotional disorders are recognised in their schools as having special educational needs (ONS 2005). This means the proportion of excluded children with mental health problems is likely closer to 100 per cent. (Institute for Public Policy Research, 2017)

Matching up to systems

In my work I place SF Coaching as a non-diagnostic, educational approach to support children experiencing any kind of distress in school, including that which emerges as challenging behaviour. Schools are familiar with coaching in general and SF Coaching gains an easier entry than SFBT. Our work is going well, exclusion is being constrained and overall the improvement is being sustained against a national background of rising rates of exclusion.

Many school staff attending my training take up SF Coaching enthusiastically and SF Coaching begins its journey into becoming routine practice in school. However, some schools are refractive and still exclude children at a high rate while other support services seem bound to a deficit focused way of working.

In the UK, training in SF Coaching has been available for many years, yet when I ask people attending my courses about their knowledge and experience of the SF approach, it is very rarely that anyone has even heard of it. SF practice was brought into the UK from the US in the late 1980s by Brief in London. I first made contact with Brief in 2001 when I was working as a behaviour support specialist teacher for a local authority and attended training with them in SFBT and SF Coaching and Supervision. At the time I was studying for my PhD, looking for a new and educational way to work with children struggling in school as an alternative to the universal reward and punishment approach, particularly when it had failed them and was leading inexorably towards exclusion. I called Brief in February 2018 and asked Evan George, one of the principals, if he could tell me about Brief's work with SF Coaching. Brief first offered training in 2001 and the number of trainees between then and now runs into the thousands, a significant number of which are school staff or in school-related professions. I asked Evan for his opinion as to why SF Coaching had not established itself in schools, despite the high-quality training offered by Brief and others over many years. His view was that the answer lies in paperwork. It seems that while the practice is sound, the paperwork in terms of written policies for the deployment of SF Coaching and the written evidence base, from academic research and published case studies of SF practice, is the weak spot.

Because of this, while SF practice is present in schools and in the schooling system in places, there is insufficient co-ordination in the collection of evidence of what works and of how it works across the field, and the lack of paperwork weakens the ability of the SF approach to gain entry to systems which prioritise evidence and structure.

I recently presented workshops on SF Coaching in school at a conference hosted by Essex County Council (ECC) with the title 'Solutions Focused Practice in Statutory Contexts'. ECC first took up SF practice in 2011 in response to rising numbers of children being taken into care in the county. I asked Loredana Grigore, Team Manager of D-BIT Mid (Divisional Based Intervention Team Service) ECC what had enabled SFBT to become established in the Service. It was clear that the commitment of a senior service manager to the approach in 2011, and sustained training and reflective practice being written into ECC policy, has been crucial.

In 2013 ECC committed to a robust evaluation of D-BIT.

The website www.workingforessex.com/our-roles/children-families carries general information on SF practice in Essex:

THE DIVISIONAL BASED INTERVENTION TEAM SERVICE (D-BIT)

This Intensive Family Support Service is designed for young people between the ages of 11 and 17 and their families, where the young person/family is considered by the local authority to be 'in crisis', and that the young person is on the cusp of a reactive care or custody episode. They use a strengths based approach to support families and prevent family breakdown. An extended team of skilled, quadrant-based staff work intensively with young people and families to identify workable solutions and help improve their relationships.

FAMILY SOLUTIONS SERVICE

The Essex Family Solutions (FS) service engages families with a range of issues on a voluntary basis for up to 12 months. Using solution focused and motivational styles of working, they help families move closer to their goals. Each team consists of a team manager, practice supervisor, family worker, assistant family worker, early intervention worker and business support.

The direct significance of the ECC experience to our thinking about SF practice in education is that D-BIT have set up a 2018 pilot project offering SFBT to schools to meet the needs of children who are known to the care team. My interest is in seeing the impact of an outside service providing a new form of support on the practices within school, able to be transferred to school staff to increase their range, and how this transfer might happen.

Compared to SF Coaching as a relatively new approach on the edge of service uptake, Signs of Safety is well known and well respected, doing vital work in a climate of increasing demand in the care services and diminishing funding, and an exploration of lessons learnt and possible clues for SFSE now follows.

Signs of success: implementing Signs of Safety within children's services worldwide

Professor Andrew Turnell, Professor Eileen Munro and Terry Murphy

The Signs of Safety is a safety-organised, solution focused approach to child protection that has evolved over the past 30 years and is now being used and implemented in jurisdictions and organisations in Europe, North America and Australasia (Turnell and Edwards, 1999; Turnell and Murphy, 2015). As the practice model has evolved, it has become increasingly clear that the major challenge to actually applying this participatory, solution focused approach with families lies in creating whole system organisational changes that can support meaningful collaboration with families. This is a particular challenge since child protection agencies across the world have become so captured by top-down managerial control internally and in their service delivery. The Signs of Safety approach has met with significant success in different places and this has always been closely linked with organisational system change purposefully aligned to the practice (Bunn, 2013; Keddell, 2011; Lwin *et al.*, 2014; Munro and Turnell, forthcoming; Salveron *et al.*, 2015; Skrypek, Idzelis and Pecora, 2015; Turnell, Munro and Murphy, 2013).

What follows provides an overview of the implementation methods that have been developed to focus carefully on what works within the international community of Signs of Safety implementing agencies. We have come to describe our framing of implementation as 'whole system, whole person' change. We use this term to underline the comprehensive organisational transformation process that is required to secure participatory practice within statutory child protection since agencies the world over have become so consumed by risk-averse managerialism. This section is based upon and adapts sections of a report we co-authored called *You Can't Grow Roses in Concrete: Action Research Final Report: Signs of Safety: English Innovations Project* (Munro, Turnell and Murphy, 2016). The 'roses' report was written to describe the findings of the Signs of Safety implementation work undertaken with ten local authorities funded through the English government's English Innovations Programme.

'Social interventions are complex systems thrust into complex systems' (Pawson, 2006, p.35). As procedural change has lost its lustre for governments and child protection systems around the world, increasing attention has been given to broader organisational functioning as a central factor in implementation success. Over the past decade, thinking about organisational transformation has been increasingly shaped by implementation science (e.g., Fixsen *et al.*, 2005, 2013) that comes from the US. Much implementation science thinking, however, focuses on simpler, linear reforms. This is at odds with the complexity pointed to in Pawson's quote above and therefore implementation science's key concepts need adapting to fit the complex and dynamic challenges that are always evident in children's services.

Implementation science is usually framed and focused on the installation of an intervention with demonstrated fidelity. By contrast, our work in researching and evolving organisational implementation strategies sets out to enable organisations to use the Signs of Safety as a vehicle to create a learning organisation that monitors how it is implementing the work, that reviews outcomes, successes and failures, and that establishes whole system participatory learning methods focused on the practice, allowing all staff to continuously adapt to change as necessary while keeping to the key principles of the approach. To achieve this, attention needs to be given to how the new way of working interacts with existing parts of the system, and how the system in turns aligns with the intervention. This is a more dynamic way of thinking about implementation than the more common static framing that implementing a social intervention is akin to installing new, more powerful petrol into the fuel tank of a motor car.

Further, the concept of 'resilience' has a different meaning once an organisation is viewed as a complex, constantly changing system. The engineering concept of resilience was developed in relation to stable systems and focused on efficiency, control, constancy and predictability. This concept is aimed at achieving a steady-state equilibrium where management and policy emphasise micro-command and control approaches. All of these features are visible in managerially driven child protection systems as well as most human services including education, policing and health. With a static concept of resilience, evaluation focuses on stable and constant elements in the system. By contrast, in a complex system, engineers have modified the concept so that resilience focuses on persistence and adaptability through absorbing and adjusting to changes by evolving adaptive structures and processes. Management and policy then emphasise the adaptive interplay between stabilising and destabilising properties, and evaluation focuses on the adaptability of the system. A useful metaphor representing these different concepts of resilience is provided by thinking about the fragility of rigid houses compared with the robustness of houses designed to sway when an earthquake hits.

Our understanding of the dynamic nature of implementation in complex systems has deepened throughout our emerging focus on implementation over the past decade and is captured in a revised framework that illustrates how implementation is a continuous learning and development cycle with the practice framework at the centre.

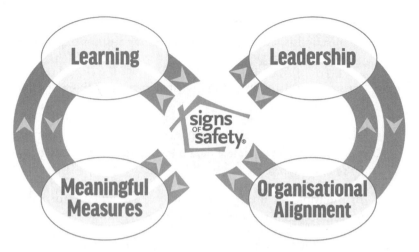

Figure 1.1: Organisation implementation framework

This framework clearly locates the Signs of Safety as the practice model in the middle of the implementation infinity loop and hence is our visual distillation of the Signs of Safety Organisational Implementation Framework. The infinity loop is used to visually underline that implementation is a continuous dynamic process. Any organisational service model or innovation could replace the Signs of Safety logo in this illustration to emphasise the essential need for full whole system engagement with the innovation for implementation to be successful.

Within children's services, as in most bureaucracies, most transformation has focused on procedures, training, measurement or leadership practice. While all these are important, this figure emphasises the centrality of the practice approach as the foundation of organisational transformation. That is why it is at the centre of the continual learning and development cycle. At its simplest we are seeking to illustrate the obvious point that everything an organisation does, its leadership, procedures, measurement and learning, must always focus on what practitioners actually do with children and families. Without an end-to-end practice approach that the organisation can align with, transformation will derail.

The key implementation activities are seen as follows:

- Learning, including core training that flows into specific continuous learning methods. It is crucial to emphasise that training, which is so often treated as the whole of an implementation programme, is seen as simply a precursor of learning.

- Leadership development that builds congruence between how the organisation is led and managed and how work is expected to occur with families.

- Organisational alignment so that structures and processes fully support the practice.

- Meaningful measurement through participatory quality assurance encompassing key practice data matched to the results logics of the practice approach.

- Information technology to provide case and performance information consistent with the practice.

The concept of 'fidelity to method' is still important but is also framed more broadly, first in focusing on fidelity to the principles and disciplines of Signs of Safety rather than solely on the specific tools or processes, and second in expecting that fidelity be apparent throughout the organisation, not just in the actions of the front-line staff.

In 2014–16 the English Innovations Project involved working with ten local authorities. Our implementation work was collaborative, seeking to form a shared understanding of the problems and co-creating solutions among all the authorities that have been faithful to Signs of Safety within the English context. This deliberately parallels the participatory approach that grounds the work between families and practitioners using the Signs of Safety practice framework. An agency's pattern of working relationships will always tend to be defined and cascade down from the top, and in England, the dominant 'command and control' approach of previous political reform efforts is thereby often duplicated in the relationships between managers and front-line workers and, in turn, between front-line workers and families (see, for example, Forrester *et al.*, 2008). The Signs of Safety approach aims to achieve respectful engagement with families, that harnesses their strengths and resources as a hopeful foundation to rigorously explore highly personal and anxiety-producing problems, and then together find solutions. Social workers will feel much more supported and able to practise in this way when they themselves experience equivalent participatory and respectful relationships with their seniors. Thus we pursue leadership where practitioners are continually engaged in learning together how to navigate the ongoing anxious environment that exists in every children's services agency.

This collaborative approach that we applied in the English Innovations Project not only helped each authority design its own implementation journey, but also was flexible enough to allow and encourage new innovations. For example:

- extending Signs of Safety from child protection work to other parts of children's services such as early help (the English name for family support services) and children in care

- developing the My Three Houses app with practitioners for working directly with children

- a participatory project to create a Signs of Safety/Wellbeing/Success IT recording system

- developing a Signs of Safety quality assurance system including participatory audit.

The English project operated with two theories of change: a practice theory of how change is produced in families and an organisational theory about the organisational environment that is required to enable and promote practice with families of the kind envisaged. Both theories of change presented below are revised from the theories that informed us at the start of the Innovations project. The revisions to both theories were made based on action learnings that emerged from the project.

The revised practice theory of change clearly distinguishes between the assessment and action cycles and is more detailed than the latter. The work undertaken in the English Innovations Project enabled us to see that the organisational theory of change we began with in 2014 focused excessively on the training, supervision and practice of front-line practitioners, almost completely overlooking organisational leadership and culture as key factors that define and shape practitioner performance and resilience. The revised organisational theory of change parallels the infinity loop implementation illustration that locates the Signs of Safety practice approach, and the principles that underpin it, as the vehicle through which whole organisation learning and improvement can be achieved.

Revised Signs of Safety practice and organisational theories of change

Children's services practitioners' ability to deliver quality, timely Signs of Safety services is always dependent on the level of support and alignment their agency provides around the practice. Therefore, the Signs of Safety practice theory of change is paired with the Signs of Safety organisational theory of change.

Signs of Safety practice theory of change

The Signs of Safety practice theory of change posits that:

> If all Signs of Safety practice methods are used by practitioners with quality and in a timely way, and this work is undertaken collaboratively with the children, parents and naturally connected support network, the child's safety will improve significantly.

The practice theory of change articulates the hypothesised goal as above and the minimum steps, or result logics, of the Signs of Safety approach to ensure it is delivered with fidelity. This constitutes what researchers call the logics model of the theory of change.

The Signs of Safety practice theory of change involves two interconnected iterative cycles: an assessment and analysis cycle and an action cycle.

Assessment and analysis cycle

The assessment and analysis cycle involves the following minimum steps:

- A referral that details concerns about a vulnerable child or young person is made to children's services. The referral usually arises from behaviours of parents or carers that are seen to be harmful to a child or young person. However, a referral can also occur because the child's or young person's behaviour is creating problems and/or is seen as dangerous to themselves or others.

- Assessment begins with the intake professional inquiring and sorting information into the Signs of Safety map under the 'What's Working', 'Worrying' and 'Needed' headings.

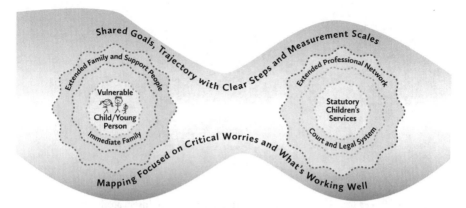

Figure 1.2: Theory of change assessment and analysis cycle

The assessment and analysis cycle steps move interactively through the three stages of assessment:

1. Information gathering

2. Analysis

3. Judgement

Child protection assessment can become bogged down in information gathering with professionals feeling too anxious to analyse and judge. The Signs of Safety assessment and analysis cycle aims for agility, asking practitioners to move quickly through all three stages. Completion is expected in around 14 days. The capacity for practitioners and their supervisors to work in this way is supported by a comprehensive framing of risk, considering strengths, existing and future safety, as well as harm and danger, and tools that support this framing alongside structured group supervision methods that build and sustain a practice culture where decision making and risk are shared. The focus throughout is on analysis, family participation and setting up the whole map and trajectory as quickly as possible, then moving into action. The action and learning from it will iteratively refine the assessment as the solutions are built with the children, family and support people always at the centre of planning and action.

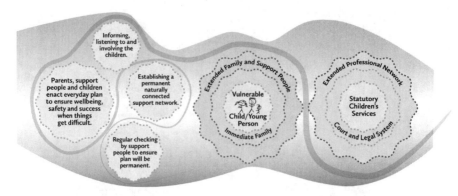

Figure 1.3: Theory of change action cycle integrated with the assessment and analysis cycle

The action cycle focuses on building the family's and network's capacity to act to ensure the child's safety when circumstances could, or do, become dangerous. The action cycle involves the following minimum steps:

- listening to, informing, and involving the children through the whole action cycle.

- finding support people and establishing them as a permanent, naturally connected support network around the immediate family

- professionals leading the parents, support people and children in developing an everyday safety plan to ensure the children will always be safe when family life could, or does, become dangerous

- parents, support people and children demonstrating they can, and will, always use the safety plan

- naturally connected support people providing a watchful eye and all support necessary to ensure the safety plan will be permanent

- professionals leading the parents, support people and children in continually thinking though their current assessment of safety.

The iterative action – assessment and analysis – cycles continue (represented diagrammatically by the interactional flows linking assessment and analysis with action) until everyone judges the safety to be high enough and permanent (usually everyone scoring seven or above on the safety scale). When this occurs, the case is closed.

Signs of Safety organisational theory of change

The Signs of Safety organisational theory of change posits that:

> When the Signs of Safety practice methods and the organisation learning, measurement, alignment and leadership methods are implemented across the whole agency, this creates a continuous organisational learning system built around the practice approach and focused on service delivery. When every tier of the organisation, from field staff to the CEO, is engaged in the learning system through position specific learning and feedback methods, the agency will secure significantly enhanced practice consistency and improved outcomes for children.

Signs of Safety implementation involves a comprehensive organisational transformation process since agencies usually have extensive entrenched and interconnected policies, processes and systems that define both direct practice and organisational culture. Aligning the organisation to enable, rather than impede, the Signs of Safety paradigm shift requires organisational change on multiple fronts. Leaders need to be alert to the reality that both organisation and staff will inevitably be caught between 'old' and 'new' policies, processes, systems and cultures. Leaders must also understand that organisational alignment takes time and concerted effort.

The Signs of Safety organisational theory of change illustrates the centrality of the practice approach as the foundation for organisational transformation. Organisational change involves continuous cycles of learning and development. As alignments that enable the practice in day-to-day work are assessed against outcomes, learning and improvement become successively focused on, and congruent with, front-line practice.

The Signs of Safety organisational theory of change and the implementation framework emphasise the continuing organisational action learning process of gathering information, setting strategies, taking action, learning from results, adjusting and starting again. The infinity loop also implies the agility and responsiveness required to lead and drive change in large organisations operating within larger human service and political systems.

At every level, leaders are managing complex and contentious work.

The organisational theory of change is illustrated as flowing directly from, and interlinked with, the practice theory of change.

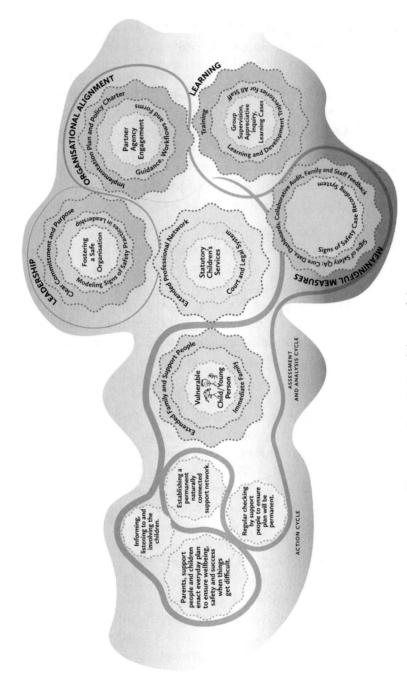

Figure 1.4: Organisational theory of change

While the organisational theory of change steps are presented here in a notionally linear fashion, in practice they are iterative and interactive.

Preparation phase

- Leadership makes a clear and explicit commitment to the implementation of Signs of Safety.

- Leadership determines a focused set of goals for adopting Signs of Safety practice, with corresponding measures, that are tested and adjusted with the workforce.

- Targeted briefings and introductions to Signs of Safety are implemented for practice leadership staff, key partners and political leadership.

- Consultation is carried out on a number of typical cases to seed the practice, create examples for the coming training, and begin whole agency learning focused on the practice.

- The implementation plan is developed, including an organisational policy or charter that describes the practice and reflects the organisational commitment and purpose.

Implementation phase

- Hold launch event and deliver strategic communications.

- Provide basic training for all staff, including leadership and key partners, with clear permission and direction to start using the practice.

- Give comprehensive briefings for partner agencies appropriate to their roles within children's services and universal services.

- Commence core data collection to measure achievement of implementation goals.

- Encourage and drive modelling of Signs of Safety practices in day-to-day leadership, including fostering a safe organisation for staff.

- Identify guidance, processes and forms that create barriers to practice.

- Remove or align these as a priority.

- Conduct first annual baseline family and staff feedback surveys.

- Commence learning and development trajectories for all leadership levels.

- Provide advanced training for practice leaders (supervisors, practice consultants), implementation leaders (service managers and quality assurance staff) and senior management.

- Practice leaders and front-line staff commence group supervision.

- Commence targeted appreciative inquiries at various levels across the organisation.

- Commence collaborative case audits.

- Introduce dashboards at team level through manual technology to monitor use of the practice approach.

- Map out work plan and ongoing process, involving front-line staff, to align workflows, guidance and forms, based on identification of barriers and what works in practice.

- Map out work plan to align the overall quality assurance (QA) processes further.

- Map out work plan and process to align IT consistent with the practice methodology and also automate dashboards to monitor the practice use at all levels.

- Continue learning and development trajectories for all levels of staff, incorporating learning from quality assurance, group supervision and appreciative inquiries.

- Continue learning case work for whole agency learning.

- Review progress. Incorporate learning from quality assurance, group supervision and appreciative inquiries. Revise implementation strategies at team, service, senior leadership level regularly and for the entire organisation annually.

The theory of change elaborated in the Signs of Safety organisational implementation framework is based on two years of intense activity within a five-year organisational commitment.

The framework sets out in more detail the various steps involved in leadership organisational alignment, learning and meaningful measures, and forms the basis for the organisation's implementation plan and review.

The implementation framework is underpinned by learning and development trajectories for all leaders within the organisation: practice leaders (supervisory level), senior leadership, service management, corporate policy and QA. The trajectories involve defined programmes of activities specifying the learning content and action learning methods for both practice skills and their leadership roles.

Organisational culture

At the heart of the Signs of Safety framework are three principles that need to be embedded in the organisational culture in order for them to be fully demonstrated in work with families. The three principles address key challenges of the work:

1. Working relationships are paramount. Relationships must enable honest and respectful discussions of concerns and worries, draw on and honour everything positive, consider multiple perspectives, and always incorporate skilful use of authority. Research shows that, irrespective of the type of intervention, professionals see better outcomes when there is shared understanding of what needs to change, agreement on purpose and goals, and family members feel their worker understands them.

2. Thinking critically and maintaining a stance of critical inquiry. In order to minimise error, a culture of shared reflective practice and a willingness to admit you may be wrong are vital. Risk assessment is a core task and requires constant balancing of strengths and dangers to avoid the common errors of drifting into an overly negative or positive view of the situation.

3. Grounded in everyday experience. Assessment and safety planning are always focused on the everyday lived experience of the child. Service recipients and front-line practitioners are

the key arbiters of whether practice works or doesn't. Evidence about the extent to which these principles are entering the organisational culture was taken from a number of sources. The primary source is the staff survey that collected people's views on how much they experienced the desired culture. In addition, focus groups, interviews and discussions at workshops added to our understanding.

Key lessons of the Signs of Safety whole system implementation framework
Creating an international learning community

Around the world, statutory children's services, at both national and local levels, have become defined by a defensive, compliance-driven culture. It takes courage to break out of this mindset, to undertake the substantial effort required to realign a child protection agency, and to develop an organisation that allows and supports workers to practise in a way that understands and accepts the complexity and uncertainty of risk decision making and management. Implementing agencies regularly report that their organisational journeys of transformation have been more confident and bold because they are operating within an international group of agencies on similar journeys. The Signs of Safety community of agencies and people, nationally and internationally, supports collective action and learning between children's services agencies and the institutions and organisations that support them. Human services agencies, indeed districts and teams within districts, tend to become siloed so that learning is diminished and particular habits of thinking and practice become entrenched. Sharing practice across organisations, as well as within organisations, is a crucial driver for developing a consensus about what good practice looks like. Importantly, too, sharing policies and procedures has encouraged agencies to extend and expand their alignment and streamlining further than they otherwise might have. To foster an international community of learning, the Signs of Safety community holds international Signs of Safety Gatherings on a yearly basis, and maintains continually updated web-based communications platforms and a digital library called the Signs of Safety Knowledge Bank. Relationships are also sustained with key tertiary and peak bodies, and partnerships with the information technology industry have been created to develop a Signs of Safety aligned information-recording system that can support implementation.

Implementation must be grounded in practice

Every Signs of Safety implementation, whether in local authorities in England, Ireland, the Flemish part of Belgium, Alberta, Missouri, Western Australia, Saitama Japan or Batambang Cambodia (these are some of the current large-scale international implementations), reaffirms to us that transformation within children's services must always be grounded in practice, specifically how practitioners actually do the direct work with children and families. The problem with so much reform endeavour within children's services, whether national reviews or local strategies, is that they tend to exclusively focus on structures and professional development without addressing the question of how the work actually gets done with families. The corollary of this has been that organisational development has by and large not engaged practitioners in the design of the reforms, and most transformation initiatives focus only minimally on how front-line work is actually practised.

Leadership

It is well understood that leadership is critical to all organisational performance. Since competency is quiet and the most effective leadership is often invisible, what constitutes effective senior leadership in children's services has perhaps been less well understood. The experience of the project has highlighted that senior management is required to understand and drive the implementation, be deliberate, agile and responsive, and not delegate the responsibility and activity. Moreover, to drive a transformation of practice demands leaders being close to the practice and understanding the approach and the experience of families and front-line staff. In the face of relentless demands on leadership, financial, organisational and political, the focus on practice requires sustained deliberate effort.

The Signs of Safety implementation framework also emphasises leadership building an organisation that creates certainty and confidence for staff that they will be supported through the anxiety, contention and crises that are inherent in child protection work. In the face of a sustained history of gratuitous blaming of individuals for poor performance and tragedies, both nationally and locally, and the high levels of anxiety that accompany the potential for tragedy in all children's service work, building safe organisations takes time and is a major culture shift in itself. Within child protection the reality is that leaders will inevitably be tested when a high-profile death occurs. For this reason we always explicitly work with leaders to prepare them to lead constructively following significant adverse incidents and fatalities. If leaders resort to a defensive, blaming response this will significantly undermine the agency and system's capacity to foster participatory practice. For this reason, we have also placed importance on documenting successful leadership practices to enable leaders to 'lead for learning following a fatality' (Turnell, Munro and Murphy, 2013).

Learning is the goal – training is exposure

The most frequent recurring error that organisations make in implementing new initiatives is to mistake training for implementation. For most staff in any implementing organisation, training will be the first step in commencing their learning journey with the Signs of Safety. It is vital that training is seen as important and is of the highest quality, but training also always needs to be viewed and messaged in its proper place, simply as exposure and the usual first step in learning. This framing of course links to Senge's thinking about creating a learning organisation (Senge, 1990). To assist organisations in creating a learning culture and a learning organisation, the Signs of Safety approach utilises the interactional 70:20:10 learning theory (Jennings, 2013) to underpin the learning component of the Signs of Safety implementation framework. The 70:20:10 model locates training in its proper place and frames learning itself as an ongoing process equally applicable to the practitioner as well as organisational leaders.

The 70:20:10 learning model posits that the smallest amount of learning comes from formal training (10%). Human beings learn in action, so in human services, most learning occurs, and habits are formed, through daily work (70%) as practitioners, supervisors and other leaders put the skills and methods into everyday practice. While the action of daily work is 70 per cent of learning and habituates how a skill is used, the pace of doing the work means most learning from action is intuitive and largely unconscious. Improvement and change require feedback and analysis through structured reflection methods. This is the critical 20 per cent of learning where the individual and group can improve by reflecting on what they are doing. To be effective, the reflection must be based on quality timely feedback.

Thus within the Signs of Safety approach we distinguish between practice methods (methods and tools used in the direct work) and learning methods. Signs of Safety learning methods include structured group supervision and appreciative inquiry processes, collaborative case audits and participatory dashboards. These provide structured continuous participatory learning processes that involve all staff from field staff to senior leadership, focus on analysis and reflection and provide clear methods to enable the organisation to actually enact the aspiration of becoming a learning organisation.

Organisational alignment

Aligning the organisation to the practice – removing blocks, enabling Signs of Safety practice though measures such as clear supporting practice guidance, procedural adjustment, group supervision, partner engagement and building resilience – is critical. The reality is that achieving organisational alignment to the practice can be slow and painful in mature organisations that have entrenched policies and procedures that pass largely unquestioned and have been built up over decades of government direction and are interlinked with critical infrastructure in quality assurance and information technology. Our experience tells us that there is no such thing as a perfect implementation; even the best organisational alignment efforts are always partial. This is especially so since there is always so much external change that constantly impacts on statutory child protection agencies.

Meaningful measures

In the past five years it has been clear to us that meaningful system alignment required us to engage actively with the 'big ticket' organisational drivers of quality assurance and information technology systems. What and how agencies and practitioners measure the information that must be recorded, and how work is assessed as satisfactory, all have a significant determining impact on practice. These systems also change more slowly than the speed at which it is possible to change the practice itself. Though these systems should monitor and enable good practice more often, they often foster a 'tick box' defensive mentality in the organisation and field staff. For this reason we have formalised our thinking about transforming quality assurance and recording systems under the rubric of 'meaningful measures'.

The Signs of Safety Participatory Quality Assurance System (Turnell and Murphy, 2015) encompasses:

- collaborative case audit, reflecting the Signs of Safety practice theory of change

- dashboard to monitor application of the Signs of Safety practice methodology in individual case management

- family and staff feedback on practice and organisational fit and leadership respectively, reflecting Signs of Safety fidelity, through annual surveys

- core data for monitoring specific goals, case trends and outcomes with a small set of key indicators that are already collected.

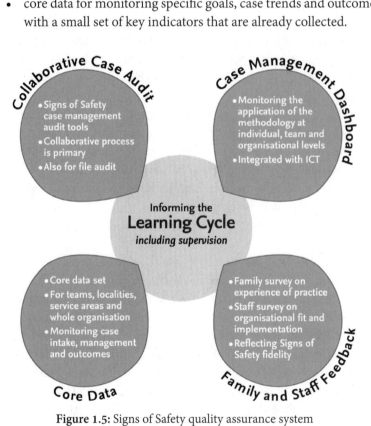

Figure 1.5: Signs of Safety quality assurance system

The Signs of Safety Participatory Quality Assurance System, first developed within the English Innovations Project, has been a substantial step towards:

- becoming clearer about what and how we measure in order to actually make a difference for children and families

- defining how measurement can be undertaken together with, rather than done to, workers and to inform the organisation.

Computer-based information-recording systems are perhaps the most significant organisational drivers of practitioner behaviour. What counts is inevitably what is counted and sadly most of what is counted doesn't count in regard to improving outcomes for children. Most of what is counted in children's services' recording systems is what can easily be counted, such as the completion of procedures, forms and the meeting of deadlines.

To rectify this, the international Signs of Safety community has partnered with a number of software development firms who focus on human and children's services to develop a Signs of Safety, Wellbeing and Success information-recording system that directly assists and guides practitioners and managers in their use of the approach from case commencement to closure. To our knowledge this is the first time a practice approach has been used to define and structure the parameters of a child protection information-recording system. While these observations can be read as an 'advertisement' for the Signs of Safety and the IT system associated with it, our point here is broader and more important. To create whole system alignment and genuinely support practice transformation, governments and agencies must connect and make their recording systems directly relevant to what workers do with families and what front-line staff know to be effective practice. Manufacturing more procedurally driven recording systems will only hollow out organisational culture and further dehumanise practice.

Whole person, whole system implementation

The Signs of Safety implementation framework recognises that children's services are very complex human services delivered in highly contested and anxious environments.

The quality, consistency and reliability of services rest ultimately on the humanity and abilities of the people delivering the services to the children and family. In addition to adopting the practice approach and aligning the organisation to enable the practice, to improve child protection services requires attention to a 'whole person' perspective.

Such a perspective aims to support the growth of the analytical, emotional, social, cultural and spiritual intelligence of all staff, focusing particularly on field and supervisory staff since they deliver the services, so they can think and act wisely as they navigate the family, practice and organisational complexities entwined in every case.

'Whole person, whole system' thinking is about connection as well as compassion. The aim must be to infuse the child protection endeavour, from the boardroom to the family's living room, with compassionate, holistic intelligence. As a close colleague who leads a large child protection system observes, I want professionals who can think and feel at the same time!

The Signs of Safety implementation framework touches all aspects of how the agency works – the leadership, learning strategies, organisational arrangements, and how the work is recorded and measured. These, as well as the practice model itself, need to be evaluated, with the ultimate arbiters of what works being the practitioners and the families.

Implementation based on the framework as set out, if truly coupled with effective action learning cycles proceeding throughout the agency, provides multiple and continuous activities through which staff can be challenged and can grow as professionals and as people to enable them to more fully own the work they undertake. A whole person, whole system approach must always be worked out with the people that it is most critically about, the service deliverers and service recipients.

Final comments
Nick Burnett

There are some significant indicators from the work on implementing Signs of Safety that give clues as to what is likely to be needed for SFSE to be adopted at a system level within education, with the overall goal of special education being very much part of the system as opposed to a 'bolt-on' to cater for those who do not 'fit'. Key clues would appear to be the importance of:

- learning, including core training that flows into specific continuous learning methods; it is crucial to emphasise that training, which is so often treated as the whole of an implementation programme, is seen as simply a precursor of learning

- leadership development that builds congruence between how the organisation is led and managed and how work is expected to occur with students and their families

- organisational alignment so that structures and processes fully support the practice

- meaningful measurement through participatory quality assurance encompassing key practice data matched to the results logics of the practice approach

- information technology to provide case and performance information consistent with the practice.

Education has a long way to go in my view but what follow are some 'sparkling moments' where practice at a school and individual level are leading the way for the system.

References

Bunn, A. (2013) Signs of Safety in England: An NSPCC Commissioned Report on the Signs of Safety Model in Child Protection. London: NSPCC.

Danermark, B., Ekstrom, M., Jakobsen, L., Karlsson, Jan Ch. (2002 in English) *Explaining Society: Critical Realism in the Social Sciences*. London and New York: Routledge.

Department for Education (2018) *Statistics: exclusions*. Available at www.gov.uk/government/collections/statistics-exclusions (accessed 29/10/2018).

Essex County Council Family Solutions Service (2013) *Family Solutions: Information for Families*. Available at www.essex.gov.uk/Publications/Documents/Family_Service_Information_for_Famalies.pdf (accessed 2/10/2018).

Fixsen, D., Naoom, S., Blasé, K., Friedman, R. and Wallace, F. (2005) *Implementation Research: A Synthesis of the Literature*. Chapel Hill: Chapel Hill University.

Fixsen, D., Blase, K., Naoom, S. and Duda, M. (2013) *Implementation Drivers: Assessing Best Practices*. Chapel Hill: Chapel Hill University.

Forrester, D., McCambridge, J. Waissbein, C. and Rollnick, S. (2008) 'How do child and family social workers talk to parents about child welfare concerns?' *Child Abuse Review*, 17, 23–35.

Institute for Public Policy Research (2017) *Making the Difference: Breaking the Link Between School Exclusion and Social Exclusion*. Available at www.ippr.org/files/2017-10/making-the-difference-report-october-2017.pdf (accessed 2/10/2018).

James, G. (2016) *Transforming Behaviour in the Classroom: A Solution Focused Guide for New Teachers*. London and New York: Sage.

Jennings, C. (2013) *The 70:20:10 Framework Explained*. Available at www.702010forum.com (accessed 2/10/2018).

Keddell, E. (2011) 'Going home: managing "risk" through relationship in returning children from foster care to their families of origin.' *Qualitative Social Work*, 11, 604–620.

Kohn, A. (1999) *Punished by Rewards: The Trouble with Gold Stars, Incentive Plans, A's, Praise and Other Bribes*. New York: Houghton Mifflin.

Lwin, K., Versanov, A., Cheung, C., Goodman, D. and Andrews, N. (2014) 'The use of mapping in child welfare investigations: a strength-based hybrid intervention.' *Child Care in Practice*, 20(1), 81–97.

Medawar, P. (2008) *Induction and Intuition in Scientific Thought*. London and New York: Routledge.

Munro, E., Turnell, A. and Murphy, T. (2016) *You Can't Grow Roses in Concrete: Action Research Final Report: Signs of Safety: English Innovations Project*. Perth: Munro, Turnell and Murphy. Available at http://munroturnellmurphy.com/eip-report (accessed 2/10/2018).

Munro, E. and Turnell, A. (forthcoming) Risk and reward: risk intelligent child protection decision making, organisation and practice.

Oakley, D.A. and Halligan, W. (2017) 'Chasing the rainbow: the non-conscious nature of being.' *Frontiers in Psychology*, November. Available at https://doi.org/10.3389/fpsyg.2017.01924 (accessed 2/10/2018).

Pawson, R. (2006) *Evidence-based Policy: A Realist Perspective*. London: Sage.

Salveron, M., Bromfield, L., Kirika, C., Simmons, J., Murphy, T. and Turnell, A. (2015) 'Changing the way we do child protection: the implementation of Signs of Safety within the Western Australian Department for Child Protection and Family Support.' *Children and Youth Services Review*, 48, 126–139.

Senge, P. (1990) *The Fifth Discipline: The Art and Practice of the Learning Organisation*. New York: Doubleday.

Skrypek, M., Idzelis, M. and Pecora, P. (2015) 'Listening to parents: lessons from implementing "Signs of Safety" in child protective services.' *Social Work Now*, 52, 29–37.

Turnell, A. and Edwards, S. (1999) *Signs of Safety: A Safety and Solution Oriented Approach to Child Protection Casework*. New York: W.W. Norton.

Turnell, A. and Murphy, T. (2015) Signs of Safety: Comprehensive Briefing Paper. Perth: Resolutions Consultancy. Available at www.signsofsafety.net (accessed 2/10/2018).

Turnell, A., Munro, E. and Murphy, T. (2013) 'Soft is hardest: leading for learning in child protection services following a child fatality.' *Child Welfare*, 92(2), 199–216.

Chapter 2

SOLUTIONS FOCUSED SPECIAL EDUCATION LEADERSHIP

Neil Birch, Nick Burnett and Dominik Godat

Introduction

Schools spend a lot of time investigating the causes of perceived underperformance within areas of the school and then set about rectifying those problems. This is potentially even more of a trap within the field of special education where an emphasis is on identifying what's 'wrong' with the individual (from the system at least) and subsequently the mindset can be on identifying difficulties experienced with a student as opposed to their strengths and abilities.

Could it be that in order to move special education to a Solutions Focused (SF) frame of reference, the leadership within the school needs to demonstrate this in its daily practice and organisation?

We believe that the leadership of a solutions-seeking organisation that plans development to achieve goals, rather than analysing failure, is the way forward in relation to Solutions Focused Special Education (SFSE). This is not to negate the importance of detailed analysis of performance and nor does it fly in the face of accountability; it simply recognises that we do not always have to 'solve' the problem in order to achieve a solution.

> *Clearly both problems and solutions do exist. However it is not always the case that they are connected or dependent on each other.*

> (Mahlberg and Sjoblom, 2004)

This chapter largely draws on the excellent work of two of the authors of this chapter: the work of Dominik Godat, who has spent time unpacking what SF Leadership more generally might be, and the research of Neil Birch which was completed for the National College of School Leadership in the UK.

It must be noted that the research was not limited only to special education settings but this chapter places the findings and discussion more centrally within a special education context. We would also want to recognise that we are not solely referring to special education in special schools but also to those who are in special education leadership positions within mainstream settings.

We then go on to explore the possible implications for SFSE leadership in schools.

The chapter finishes with a case study showing the evolving SF practices within Neil's school and practical examples of the use of policies and practices to support this.

An overview of SF Leadership

As a starting point for the discussion on leadership within SFSE we will first explore the work of Dominik, who has been involved in a two-year research project called 'From SF Leadership towards a descriptive model'.

Results and findings from the project were based around the following elements:

- descriptive model of SF Leadership

- SF Leadership behaviour, aims and supporting factors

- SF Leadership success stories in various settings

- differences between SF Coaching and SF Leadership.

From Dominik's research it was identified that SF Leadership is an ongoing interaction between:

- leaders

- employees

- stakeholders

with each of these groups acting in supportive ways to bring about the desired outcomes of:

- better results

- different behaviour

- better feelings.

The research has also identified a number of SF interactions that bring about these desired outcomes as shown below:

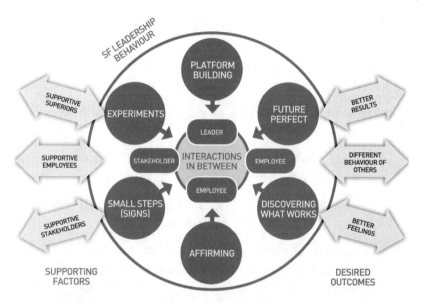

Figure 2.1: A model of SF leadership
Source: Godat (2013)

SF Coaching and approaches generally are about the individual the coach/therapist is working with, whereas in a leadership role this may not always be possible or appropriate.

The analysis of the research identified four differences between SF Coaching and SF Leadership (see Table 2.1).

Table 2.1: Four differences between SF Coaching and SF Leadership

SF Leadership	SF Coaching
1. Ongoing interactions	1. One- or two-time interaction
2. The leader with own interest at stake	2. The coach supporting client's goals
3. Wide spectrum of applications	3. SF coaching session
4. Fostering SF behaviour in between employees	4. Focusing on the interaction in between the coach and the client

Before briefly exploring the second and third elements identified in Table 2.1 it is probably helpful to unpack a commonly used SF concept called 'Future Perfect' as this has not been done anywhere else and yet has become widely used by many in the SF field.

It was invented by Paul Z. Jackson and Mark McKergow for the first *The Solutions Focus* book (2007). They were looking for good names for the tools and they thought that Future Perfect was a good name for several reasons:

1. It's much snappier than 'goal' and also different – a FP is not a goal, more an aspiration.

2. Future Perfect is a way of looking at the future with everything working (i.e. perfect?).

3. Future Perfect is a tense in grammar – 'I will have done…' – which is standing in the future looking back, as one does with the FP tool.

4. We wanted to get away from 'miracle' – a miracle is one way to launch a FP conversation but there are others.

5. Some other SF people were using (and still use) 'preferred future'. To Mark, this sounded utterly wet and weedy – 'would you like sugar in your tea' is a preferred future, not the amazing dive into something new that characterises an FP conversation.

(McKergow, 2018)

It became clear from the research that creating a Future Perfect for people in a leadership role could take one of four possible areas of focus:

- Future Perfect of the organisation

- Future Perfect of the leader

- a shared Future Perfect

- individual Future Perfects.

It should also be noted that these are not mutually exclusive and more than one of these can be operating at any one time depending on the nature of the organisation and leadership required. Additionally, all four can be relevant at the same time and mutually influence each other. More information as to how these might operate is identified in Figure 2.2.

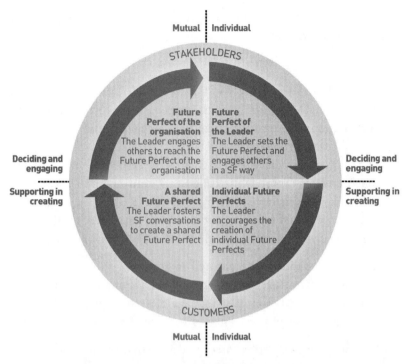

Figure 2.2: Four Future Perfects in SF Leadership
and the behaviour of the leader
Source: Godat (2013)

Future Perfect of the organisation

The focus here is on the co-creation of a Future Perfect with relevant stakeholders. In this position the leader is of an equal footing in the development of the Future Perfect with the team of stakeholders brought together to create the organisational Future Perfect.

Benefits of adopting this approach are very much in the ownership of the Future Perfect by those involved in the process. Challenges could be in bringing together what might be very different viewpoints. There are a number of SF resources and methodologies that can bring this about.

One such approach developed by Paul Z. Jackson and shared in detail in *57 SF Activities for Facilitators and Consultants* (Röhrig and Clarke, 2008), is 'Future Perfect: Documentary'. This is described as a lively and memorable way for a team to think about, articulate and capture their collective Future Perfect. In short, the team members get to describe a 10 on their scale or to picture their answer to the 'Miracle Question', both common SF techniques.

Future Perfect of the leader

The focus, quite clearly, here is on the leader's view of Future Perfect for the organisation. The key to staying SF and engagement is then how the leader engages stakeholders in a SF way.

One approach we have seen used effectively in combining the first approach and this approach is called the Solution Focused Strategy Canvassing. This was developed by Adie Shariff and Alison Abington (2010), and we would refer you to the original case study for the detail. In short, two central principles underpin the Canvas approach:

1. Strategy needs to be defined in terms of value delivered to customers or stakeholders, and in SFSE the students and possibly parents. In this way the language of strategy is simplified and described in a way that enables a shared view of success.

2. Strategy is best represented in a single picture so that it can be communicated simply and rapidly and can be reviewed with frequency and ease at all levels to ensure focused collective effort in making strategy happen.

Developing a Canvas with a group will typically involve engagement with the following three sets of questions:

1. Detailing a preferred future – based on the leader's best hopes and the difference this would make:

    i.   What does our strategic success look like to our students and parents?

    ii. In what ways will interactions between staff, students and parents be different?

    iii. Will whom we are interacting with be different?

2. Identifying scales that underpin the preferred future:

    i.   What are the five to eight 'critical success factors' (high-level aspirational objectives) that we must deliver on to have any chance of strategic success?

ii. Is each scale ('critical success factor') absolutely necessary to our success?

iii. Are they collectively sufficient to enable success?

3. Graphing and multiple scaling:

i. On a scale of '0' to '10', how would we know we were at '10' on each 'critical success factor'?

ii. Where are we on each scale at present?

iii. What puts us at each respective score?

iv. Where is 'good enough' for us, and for other tiers of management?

v. What would be signs of progress on each scale?

In the case study shared in the article by Shariff and Abington, the following benefits to using this approach were identified by a senior leader:

- team alignment

- purpose and creativity

- common language and shared vision

- ownership and empowerment

- control and freedom.

The key to any SF approach is being responsive to the context and so the development and implementation of a Strategy Canvas would be highly individualised but having a process can be useful in what is a very complex area.

A shared Future Perfect

The focus of this position is similar to the ones just shared with the major difference being who is involved in creating the Future Perfect and how they are involved. It may well be appropriate for the relevant stakeholders (parents, governors, community members) to be fully involved as described in the 'Future Perfect of the organisation' section.

However, it may be more appropriate to include stakeholders through holding a range of SF conversations to better understand what their view of Future Perfect would be, and to then draw on these conversations in either the leader framing the Future Perfect, or in all team members sharing their insights from the conversations.

Individual Future Perfects

This position is most closely aligned with SF Coaching and could be developed alongside or separate from the organisation Future Perfect. We are of the view that it is likely to be appropriate for these individual Future Perfects to be in some way aligned with the organisation Future Perfect.

Applications of SF Leadership

As was also identified in the differences between SF Leadership and SF Coaching, there is a wide spectrum of applications that SF Leadership encompasses. The research identified the following six areas and this is expanded in Figure 2.3.

- SF Everyday Interactions
- SF in Leadership Tools
- SF in Meetings
- SF Coachings
- SF in Workshops
- SF in Management Cycles

SF Everyday Interactions

Having not only leaders but all staff trained in SF approaches would enable everyday interactions to be grounded in SF. Leaders having a good knowledge of SF tools and approaches is a useful starting point, and there will be more about this in the case study at the end of the chapter.

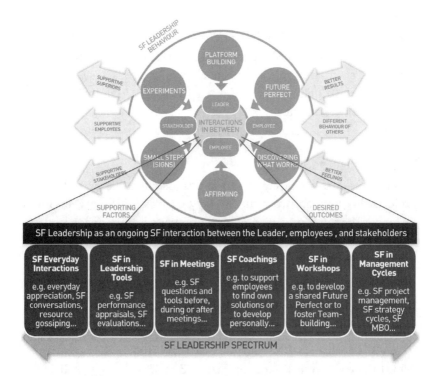

Figure 2.3: Wide spectrum of SF Leadership applications
Source: Godat (2013)

SF in Leadership Tools

This will be explored in Chapter 4. In brief, the SF approach needs to be built into all processes as well as just the everyday interactions; otherwise there is a disconnect for staff between what is said and what is done.

SF in Meetings

This will be explored in Chapter 5, and as with 'SF in Leadership Tools', this is about walking the talk, and ensuring that what all leaders do is strongly SF influenced.

SF Coachings

This will be explored in Chapter 4 as a key component for supporting and developing staff.

SF in Workshops

The case study at the end of the chapter will reference the use of external consultants to bring a SF approach to workshops. Whether run by internal or external people, professional learning needs to sit within the SF paradigm to help connect and reinforce the 'dots' for all within the school environment.

SF in Management Cycles

This links back to the Strategy Canvas discussions earlier as well as any projects that flow out from the Strategy Canvas for the organisation. Ensuring they are built on SF foundations and approaches leads to greater overall impact for the organisation and all who come into contact with the organisation.

From Dominik's ongoing work we will now share a suggested competency framework.

SF Leadership Competence Framework

Whilst there are some (many) in the world of SF who might balk at the idea of a competency framework, we believe it can be useful to help both current and aspirant leaders identify current and future behaviours that would suggest they are implementing SF Leadership.

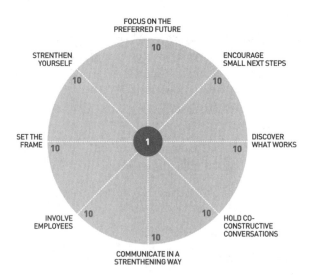

Figure 2.4: SF Leadership competencies

SF leaders...

Focus on the preferred future

- elaborate a realistic description of the preferred future with their employees instead of analysing problems or the past

- ask 'What do you want instead?' when employees say what they don't want

- see problems as a preferred future that is not yet achieved.

Encourage small next steps

- elaborate small next steps with their employees instead of working out action plans

- ask employees for motivating small next steps that they can realise with confidence

- explore signs of progress with their employees.

Discover what works

- give their employees feedback about functioning behaviour

- build solutions on what already works

- create a platform where employees, teams and the organisation can learn from success stories.

Hold co-constructive conversations

- build conversations on deliberately chosen words of the employees

- describe circumstances with interactional terms instead of stabilising concepts (such as character traits)

- use solution focused questions as the main means of communication.

Communicate in a strengthening way

- give appreciation for concrete behaviour

- foster an appreciative climate amongst their employees

- express and radiate confidence.

Involve employees

- motivate employees asking SF questions instead of telling them their 'solution'

- foster the responsibility of employees with SF questions

- promote the integration of ideas from many employees.

Set the frame

- communicate when SF questions are appropriate and when something else is needed

- express expectations and goals clearly

- enrich classic leadership tools with SF ideas.

Strengthen themselves

- exchange with other SF practitioners

- win like-minded people inside the company

- set a SF example and strengthen themselves with their own enthusiasm and the excitement of others.

A possible way of implementing this could be for the individual (and others) to rate themselves on a scale of 1–10 in relation to each of the competencies…what gets them that high…what would take them one step higher…or…what does 10 look, sound, feel like.

Review of SF Leadership

As the wide-ranging backgrounds of participants in the research show, SF Leadership not only works very well in various situations and can be applied in almost any setting, but also fits a dynamic and challenging environment.

As the world of special education certainly fits the bill as dynamic and challenging, it would seem that the developing model of SF Leadership could provide some clues as to the type of SFSE system leadership needed to bring about systemic change.

The final word on SF Leadership in general goes to one of the participants in Dominik's SF Leadership Survey who summarises this approach as being about 'skipping the maze of problems and finding new creative and simple ways'.

SF and school leadership

School leadership is really a matter of leading the conversation by shaping and reframing key concepts, purposes, relationships, observations, evaluations, possibilities, processes...all strengthened by the stories told about the school and its people.

Responsibility for school leadership frequently resides with principals and senior staff and it is fairly natural for staff to attend to the contributions that senior staff members make to the ongoing conversations within the school.

Consequently, SF School Leadership requires three things:

1. A sound knowledge of SF approaches

2. Extensive participation in the life and work of the school

3. The capacity to engage in, and shape, the everyday conversations occurring in the life and work of the school.

Findings from the research into SF School Leadership

The research undertaken by Neil locates solution focused working within the context of strategic leadership, learning-centred leadership and distributed leadership models (Birch, 2007). It argues that the gap between the leader's vision for the school and the commitment of all staff to achieving this vision is where many organisations become culturally unstuck. All the schools within the study had developed their own approaches to closing this gap with different interpretations about how solution focused working could help them do so. It is felt that the solution focused approach, based on constructive dialogue and goal-setting at an individual and group level, gives a number of tools to enable staff to be involved in designing and achieving the vision.

It is clear that tools will be less effective if they are not applied within a positive culture. With education systems focused on the analysis of pupil performance results and league tables, many leaders and staff are fearful of being identified as failing. An additional issue within the field of special education is how we measure achievement as opposed to attainment, where the former is more focused on what is relevant to the individual and the latter on particular milestones. Whilst measuring attainment is important, to measure successes within special education by this alone would paint an inaccurate and unfair picture, as for some students, and their staff, achievements may mean ensuring skills are not lost or their loss is slowed down.

An issue facing school leaders is how to foster a culture of success where they and their staff are confident to put their head above the parapet. From the research the following were identified as necessary prerequisites:

- commitment and collaboration

- tools

- relationships.

It is to each of these elements that we will now turn to discuss in more detail in relation to special education.

Commitment and collaboration

All schools within the study reflected on the need for the Senior Leadership Team to be committed to adopting a SF approach. The use of many of the tools for encouraging staff contribution can quickly be negated if staff believe their contribution is not appreciated; there is the risk of criticism that the Senior Leadership Team is paying lip service to consultation. Having a member of the Senior Leadership Team driving school improvement in a solution focused way appears to be a successful approach to incorporating personal and team goals into school improvement.

Staff collegiality in the decision-making process has led to a greater diversity of ideas for all aspects of school improvement. Where staff are able to develop their own solutions to the issues facing them and the school as a whole, it was clear that they felt a greater commitment to those solutions.

SFSE leaders in schools need to 'walk the talk' and not just 'talk the talk'. Whilst this is not different if you wish to have a positive impact on any school culture, the challenge in special education is to not get drawn into discussions focused on problems and difficulties in a paradigm that is deficit focused at source.

Applying solution focused tools

Many of the tools used in solution focused working are directly applicable to whole-school improvement. The use of four specific solution focused tools was fundamental to the success of the approach in the schools studied. These approaches were evident in varying degrees in different school contexts. The four tools are:

- *Exception finding:* identifying those times when success was achieved. Using this tool as a structural part of team meetings was found to be effective in helping identify strategies for future success rather than analysing failure.

- *Celebrating progress:* recognising the small steps taken to achieve the overall goal. People at all levels of responsibility felt that recognising the little things they have done towards strategic whole-school goals helped those goals to stay alive during the year. Schools felt that frequently revisiting these goals during team meetings secured a greater commitment to their achievement.

- *Scaling:* using scales to measure progress towards the goal. This was felt to be very important for allowing staff to take ownership of their progress and improvement. Where scales were used frequently in staff meetings to identify 'where on the scale are we now', 'where do we want to be' and 'how do we get there', staff felt not only a sense of ownership of the goal but that they had a direct influence on achieving it.

- *Picturing preferred futures:* goal-setting to identify where you want to be in 12 months' time. Where schools adopted this approach to goal-setting it appeared that not only did the goals become clearer but also all staff felt positive about their achievement rather than negative about perceived failures to date.

Valuing relationships

One of the overriding themes from all those interviewed was the notion that by incorporating solution focused methodologies in meetings, staff appeared to believe that peer relationships had improved and there was a greater sense of shared purpose. In addition, staff also stated that they had a greater appreciation of the work and successes of other members of staff.

Feeling valued is difficult to quantify. However, phrases such as 'we enjoy working here', 'I feel I am accepted as a person' and 'staff are happy to come to work' kept reoccurring throughout the interviews with staff at all levels of all organisations.

Having worked in a range of school settings we would suggest that those working in special education generally have an increased awareness of the importance of relationships but there always remains opportunities to develop this further.

Conclusion

There are a number of key points coming out of the research and discussion which will be explored in more detail in subsequent chapters, namely the areas around staff organisation and development.

So, in summary, we believe there is a lot to commend in adopting a SFSE leadership in schools approach. We have identified below what we believe are the key messages.

Key messages

- Where the SFSE leader demonstrates a belief in staff by allowing them the opportunity to find their own solutions to issues, commitment to improvement appears to be greatly enhanced.

- Recognising the strengths of staff appears to allow SFSE school leaders opportunities to build positive solutions in collaboration with them.

- Solution focused tools allow a framework for collaboration and potentially give staff a number of 'skills' in managing team and department interactions.

- Solution focused working formalises opportunities for staff to feel their contribution is valued and enhances relationships in a mutually supportive school ethos.

- Any of the three elements of commitment, tools and relationships can be successful in bringing about school improvement, but all three in partnership give the greatest potential for success.

We will now go on to share a case study of how SFSE school leadership can be implemented.

CASE STUDY: **SF SCHOOL LEADERSHIP IN ACTION**

Neil Birch

Background

I first started working with solution focused practitioners whilst I was at the school for students with moderate learning difficulties in Dover in the early 2000s when I undertook the initial 'Picturing preferred futures' research piece with the National College for Teaching and Leadership. Developing true ownership of all aspects of the school's performance, and ensuring that everyone understood their contribution to achieving better outcomes for all, appeared to make perfect sense, particularly when working in such tight-knit learning communities as special schools. As with all good solution focused practice we have developed many networking opportunities with practitioners in other fields to share, to co-operate, to collaborate and to build commitment towards building a better solution focused school environment.

The Beacon Folkestone is a 3–19 special school for 374 students with profound severe and complex needs. The school was formed in September 2016 from the merger of two special schools (Foxwood and Highview) into a single educational provision within a brand-new purpose-built school building. The building also contains a multi-agency support hub containing health service pediatricians, therapists and social services colleagues alongside our own multi-agency team. The school also hosts the district's 'Specialist teaching and learning team', providing training advice and support for young people with additional needs in mainstream settings and supporting schools to build capacity with staff to meet their needs.

Throughout the years of the development of the Beacon we have used solution focused practice to support our work on many levels. Initially, building on the research piece 'picturing preferred futures', in 2007, through the federation of the two schools in 2009 and on into the design of the single provision, we incorporated solution focused principles in our work. Throughout, we worked closely with the Brief Institute in London and were fortunate to engage experts Evan George and Harvey Ratner from the Institute in our work.

Approach

We started this journey with a joint training day for all 290 staff (in all honesty not all of whom thought the concept of a single school was a good one!) working with Evan George and Harvey Ratner of the Brief Institute in London to begin the development of shared ethos, values, vision and culture. To take us forward from individual schools to a stronger better organisation that brought about better outcomes for its young people we knew we needed to build ethos first. Rather than asking 'How do you feel about the single school?' or even 'What do we need to do to make the new school successful?' we opened our training day with the question 'List 30 things you do well that make you confident about the Beacon's future'.

From a simplistic but deliberate change in the use of language, we have been able to build an individualised approach to learning and a collaborative and positive learning culture across the school.

Over the years we have developed a wide range of techniques and strategies for supporting the development of solution focused working across the school. Fundamentally, however, we have looked to develop a whole-school approach to collaborative improvement, using the simple and basic tenets underpinning solution focused working of:

- If it ain't broke – don't fix it.

- Once you know what works, do more of it.

- If it's not working, do something different.

Whilst we increasingly apply these principles on a small-group and an individual level with our students, we have been developing whole-school approaches in our school improvement work at a team, department and individual staff level. Our belief is that in order to be successful we have to ensure solution focused principles are embedded at all levels of the organisation. All senior leaders have undertaken solution focused leadership training and embed tools and principles when introducing or developing any piece of work alongside staff. This means that in all of our work, from identifying individual programmes to launching whole-school initiatives and from engaging in self-reflection and evaluation to peer review of the quality of teaching and learning, we incorporate the tools of scaling and exception finding as we look to identify key moments to use stepping stones towards our preferred futures.

Within the school now we use solution focused tools within our team and departmental meetings and as a formal part of reflective practice. We have developed an 'Improving Learning Framework' (see Appendix 1) which uses coaching, training, networks of support and staff reflection to underpin colleagues' ability to take their practice forward. This utilises solution focused tools to support staff on an individual and small-group basis (examples are given in Appendices 2, 3 and 4). These examples are far from 'best practice' modelling and are provided within the spirit of open and honest sharing of practice inherent within the SF community. They are real examples of where we have used a solution focused approach to reflect upon and develop our practice at all levels of leadership through the school. Simplicity is genius, or so they say, and these examples are both simple and practical! Collaboration, dialogue and the effective use of solution focused strategies are bringing about a real sense of ownership, not only of pupil progress, but also of whole-school improvement.

The future

The school is developing a strong research base to its work and within one recent Masters level study a member of staff was interviewed for their views. Their response was heartening for the future! 'Negativity is contagious and destructive – positive people are productive, fulfilled and happy. We have a positive ethos that empowers groups and individuals to problem solve and develop better solutions.'

The study also found that 98 per cent of staff believe that solution focused principles are embedded and having a distinct impact on both promoting positive behaviour and learning of pupils and in collaborative working and sharing of what's going well within and across the different teams/departments.

SF approaches provide an ideal framework within which schools can develop their practice. In designing the 'Self-improving School System', Hargreaves (2010) recognises the need for leaders who are 'morally committed to imaginative and sustainable ways of achieving more ambitious and better outcomes'. We are utilising solution focused approaches at a single team level, through to the whole school and beyond to networks of support and leadership, to cement our moral commitment to each other and to strive for more ambitious and better outcomes for our young people.

Appendix 1: The Beacon, Folkestone Improving Learning Framework

This framework identifies the use of coaching, training, networks of support and staff reflection to underpin colleagues' ability to take their practice forward.

Outline

The school's strategic intents focus on improving learners' outcomes through the delivery of high-quality teaching facilitated by high-performing teams; through engaging in an assessment for learning and improving progress culture; and through ensuring appropriate school and multi-agency support strategies assist in improving learning and sustaining progress over time for all. We believe that the practice of individuals improves within a culture of feeling valued and supported and, to this end, we have identified four cornerstones which we believe are the foundations for improving learning and performance.

All employees have a duty to ensure that our pupils receive the very best education and reach their individual potential. In order to ensure that this is happening, there has to be an element of 'quality control' or 'monitoring'. However, we have chosen to move away from the use of a 'monitoring policy' to adopt an 'improving learning' framework, with the emphasis on support as opposed to inspection. The Senior Leadership Team believes that well-trained and well-supported staff are well equipped to form high-performing teams who will enable the best outcomes for our pupils.

The Senior Leadership Team places much importance on staff wellbeing and has an 'open-door' policy whereby staff are encouraged to share any problems they may be experiencing both in and out of school. The Senior Leadership Team endeavours to be compassionate and to offer any support needed to help individuals through difficult times in both their personal and professional lives.

We have identified four cornerstones to the framework:

- training
- coaching
- support
- monitoring.

The school is split into three zones. These are semi-autonomous learning communities that function independently within the school as a whole. In this way we are able to create three smaller, more manageable, cohorts where teaching can be focused more closely on the learning needs of different cohorts of young people. In general terms (although there are some students working outside chronological year group due to their particular needs and abilities) Zone 1 consists of nursery to Year 6 pupils, Zone 2 is Years 7 to 9 plus distinct classes providing specialist teaching provision, and Zone 3 contains our Year 10 to Year 14 students (students with special needs are entitled to full-time education to the age of 19 so there is a three-year post-16 provision, which runs to Year 14).

Leaders of Learning (the school's middle leadership team distributed through each zone with responsibility for the quality of learning and pupil progress) have a key role in turning the school's vision into reality and have created their own unique approaches through collaborations within their zones.

Children in the Early Years Foundation Stage and Key Stage 1 are encouraged to explore, take risks, enjoy facing challenges, engage in open-ended activity and problem solve. With the support of sensitive and responsive adults our children are supported to become resilient, capable, confident and self-assured. We encourage our children to be aware of their own goals, make plans and review their own progress and achievements. We aim to establish a dynamic professional learning community within our zone and in collaboration with other schools that is committed to practitioner-led, inquiry-focused and evidence-based research.

Zone 2 strives to provide engaging and challenging learning experiences inside and outside the classroom, providing children with experiences that develop resilience, ambition, wellbeing, and encourage a life-long love for learning. We seek to nurture curiosity and creativity through an inspiring, engaging and rigorous curriculum. The skills students have learnt in Zone 1 are further enhanced to promote independence and personal growth, preparing students for the next phase of their education in Zone 3.

In Zone 3 our mission is to inspire and empower all individuals to fulfil their individual ambitions and goals to enable them to be active and successful citizens. Students and staff work within a safe, welcoming and stimulating environment, which embraces diversity and promotes respect. We aim to equip all students with the knowledge, skills and qualifications they need for the future to ensure that they succeed academically and become responsible, informed citizens who can make positive contributions to our global society.

Coaching

Active research enables us to be developing skills that are as up to date as possible and brings them into the school environment. All staff are encouraged to keep building on their path of professional development through continuous reflective practice and a key part of this process is sharing findings with colleagues across the school and beyond.

We are active members of this wider Kent community of special schools and aim to ensure that all staff have access to current and completed research projects and feel proud in celebrating their achievements!

The Beacon promotes coaching for improvement as a means of improving learning and performance. We use both formal and informal coaching for improvement, which is available to all staff.

- All teachers and high-level teaching assistants (HLTAs) will receive formal training in coaching.

- All HLTAs are responsible for supporting a 'hub' of teaching assistants (TAs), in which opportunities to have coaching conversations are given to all members of the hub. The HLTA acts as a mentor for new or less experienced TAs and helps with the induction process.

- All teaching staff will be allocated a mentor during their first year in post. The mentor will support the teacher with day-to-day practices and procedures as well as highlighting training needs. The mentor will signpost the teacher towards any other sources of support, for example, subject specialism or behaviour management.

- Informal coaching occurs when members of staff identify a peer whom they respect and trust and have a coaching conversation at a mutually agreed time. Teachers are encouraged to coach and observe each other teaching throughout the year or during 'peer support week' three times per year. There is an allocation within Directed Time (a designated time allocation) to enable weekly coaching.

- Formal coaching is when members of the Middle or Senior Leadership Team coach a member of staff who has specifically asked for such support or whose performance is giving concern and coaching becomes part of the support package offered.

- Formal coaching also takes place during the mid-year review and when giving feedback following a drop-in visit or lesson observation.

- Teachers are strongly encouraged to share and record their own teaching using our digital recording technology and to invite a colleague to watch the video and have a coaching session. We believe that it is good practice to become a reflective practitioner who is constantly seeking to improve, and the use of video will promote opportunities for self-reflection and self-review.

- The Senior Leadership Team is currently considering the notion of identifying Lead Coaches who will be known to all staff.

- All members of the Senior Leadership Team access coaching for improvement from colleagues in other schools.

Training

The Beacon places great emphasis on Continual Professional Development (CPD). CPD enables staff both to improve their own performance within the classroom and to contribute to the wider development of the whole school. The Senior Leadership Team will ensure that appropriate training is available to all staff. It may be composed of a combination of the following elements:

- All members of staff receive a core induction package which informs new staff of the day-to-day policies and procedures, the core values, safeguarding procedures, manual handling training and health and safety. This is supported by awareness training, which includes training in a consistent and agreed approach to managing behaviour, training in managing the needs of pupils with ASD, physical/sensory/communication needs; the use of Makaton signing and curriculum/teaching methods.

- The appraisal process supports staff to identify their own training needs. Other opportunities are signposted throughout the year by the Senior Leadership Team and requests made by individuals will also be considered if they link to the School Improvement Plan; all staff will have access to their own electronic training records to highlight progress towards targets.

- Training may be delivered in-house or by external providers both locally and nationally. We use mainstream providers for courses such as the Outstanding Teacher Programme to develop the expertise of all staff.

- Training can take many different forms: it may be subject-based or it may relate to other aspects of the development of our pupils.

- Staff are encouraged to contribute to the wider development of the school and are encouraged to take the lead on projects and initiatives, with appropriate training being made available.

- Staff are encouraged to seek promotion and to become leaders such as HLTAs, Leaders of Learning or Senior Leaders and they are supported in accessing relevant training to help with their personal development goals.

- We have identified four levels of CPD:

  Level 1 – induction training for all staff

  Level 2 – entitlement training (free training led by our own expert staff) for all staff to attend if they are able; they are encouraged to do so

  Level 3 – professional development training identified through the appraisal process

  Level 4 - professional pathways including degree/MA courses, NQTs, leadership pathways/qualification credit framework – Level 2/3 and HLTA status.

- Level 3 and 4 CPD is likely to include action research linked to improving learning outcomes.

- The use of digital technologies allows lessons to be recorded. This not only enables evidence-based personal reflection but also, with the teacher and TAs' consent, can be used for training purposes.

- Digitally recorded 'Good Practice' evidence will be used in CPD training.

- Senior leaders have been trained in observing lessons and giving feedback and they will support Leaders of Learning to develop expertise in observing lessons.

- Training and development is further enhanced by the Training and Development Focus Group.

- Teaching and Learning Alliance projects are offered to all staff to foster an environment of continuous learning and professional development.

Support

We believe that we have an extensive pool of talent to share. The expertise of individuals will be used to support those with less experience and knowledge through coaching, training and opportunities to share good practice. We will offer the following support as required.

- Peer support weeks, during which teachers record lessons using the digital recording system and watch trusted colleagues' lessons, will be offered as outlined above. Teachers are encouraged to coach each other for improvement.

- Learning walks around the school to observe the environments created by colleagues and share good practice can be carried out.

- Opportunities to watch colleagues teach and to gain new ideas will be given.

- Opportunities to observe teachers recognised as consistently outstanding in the impact of their practice in other special or mainstream schools will also be offered.

- 'Champions' may be identified, such as an ASD champion, a behaviour management champion or a Makaton champion, who make themselves available to offer coaching, advice or support to other colleagues. These 'champions' will also offer training to colleagues in order to upskill others.

- A need for some form of support may be identified from drop-in visits.

- An audit of staff skills and expertise will be made available across the Beacon in order to share expertise and offer support to colleagues.

- Focused learning walks will be undertaken by the Leaders of Learning/Senior Leadership Team and governors to provide feedback and identify areas for support.

- Professional support meetings will be held to ensure that staff are on track to meet their appraisal targets and to identify any other support needed; this is aided by software programme FILIO.

- Professional support meetings will also be held to ensure that staff feel supported within their tutor role and that any concerns about behaviour management or other pupil concerns are addressed in a supportive manner.

- External agencies can offer support and supervision as required.

- The Wellbeing Committee and Staff Social Group exist to provide mutual support.

Monitoring

Monitoring is the means by which the Senior Leadership Team ensures that teaching and learning is of the highest quality. Staff wellbeing is paramount to this and is achieved through the supportive framework outlined above. The Senior Leadership Team is responsible for the quality of teaching, learning and standards across the Beacon and the following methods will be used to ensure that these are of the highest standard:

- The governing body holds the Senior Leadership Team to account for the standards of teaching and learning. To do this, they may observe lessons, conduct learning walks and hold regular meetings with the Senior Leadership Team.

- Professional development meetings are held with the Senior Leadership Team to monitor the quality of subject improvement plans and schemes of work.

- Assessment data is regularly analysed to ensure that pupils make at least good rates of progress.

- Pupil progress meetings are held to discuss the rates of progress made by pupils, both long term and during the past 12 weeks. Good and outstanding rates of progress are celebrated while pupils causing concern are highlighted for discussion about how underachievement can be addressed.

- Learning walks are undertaken by the wider leadership team to ensure that learning environments are of the highest quality and to address any concerns.

- Moderation takes place regularly both within the school and across other KSENT (Kent Special Education Needs Trust) schools and working in partnership with mainstream schools to ensure accuracy of teacher assessment.

- Throughout the year members of the wider leadership team will regularly work with staff to support the development of their practice through a wide variety of means including:

  » regularly check that work is differentiated appropriately, that there is obvious progression during the year and that appropriate records are kept; if written work is produced, the Senior Leadership Team will monitor whether marking adheres to the marking policy and is developmental in nature and whether work is generally completed; it will often be appropriate to have video or photographic evidence of work where pupils have limited literacy skills

  » look at pupils' files to ensure that these are kept up to date with relevant information

  » regularly 'drop in' to classes and may make notes to celebrate examples of good practice which might be shared with others and to highlight any concerns; any notes made will be shared and feedback given

  » carry out formal lesson observations three times per year, and provide written feedback. We believe that the procedures and processes outlined above will ensure that we have a culture of confidence and support in which all staff strive to ensure that all pupils make rapid progress and attain the best possible outcomes, knowing that they themselves are well supported and valued.

Appendix 2: Improving Learning

This document is the frame we (Leaders of Learning and senior leaders) used to craft all elements of the Improving Learning Framework over a series of five sessions. It helped colleagues promote positive dialogue to establish principles of practice that are formalised in the final Improving Learning Framework. It formed the basis for discussion of our key areas of practice that were seen as working well as well as highlighting some specific next steps.

Where are we now?
Scale of 1 to 10 where 1 is 'We have a culture of inspection and fear' and 10 is 'All staff feel appropriately supported to improve the quality of learning'
1   2   3   4   5   6   7   8   9   10

What are our Core Values around this area?

What do we currently do well to support improvement in Teaching and Learning?

What are the key elements we want to incorporate?

What will it look like?

How we will we support its development?

Action / Next Steps

Action	By Whom	By When

Appendix 3: Reflection Tool

Leaders of Learning reflection – May 2017			
What are we now	**What is working**	**What else do we know**	**What can we do more of**
We had an introductory session to allow open and honest reflection. This built the trust in the group that stating the reality of the situation was OK. *Often within a group of middle leaders working with senior leaders there can be an atmosphere of 'say the right thing to impress the boss'!!* *It was important for us to build on what was already a strong relationship to set the context for an honest review.*	*We had developed a wide range of strategies that sometimes felt like every conversation had to be a formal SF conversation.* *This phase of our work encouraged peer questioning around not only what was happening but also its quality and impact.*	*Since the inception of our work, its context had changed alongside the changing landscape within our school. The growth of our provision brought with it other avenues and opportunities for SF working.* *This was our chance to capture this work and build it coherently into our reflections.*	*Based on the SF principles of doing more of what works we were able to build some key improvement and development points.* *Having engaged in this process we were able to build some concrete steps to improving our provision.*

This document was a reflection from the Leaders of Learning on the impact of the coaching element of the framework. Although a simplistic frame, it allowed reflection to sow the seeds of the 'next wave of development' and it allowed us to move forward quickly toward a deeper discussion around coaching and mentoring and the role and purpose of each.

Appendix 4: Senior Leadership Authentic Leadership Tool

As part of the Senior Leadership Team's work on 'authentic leadership' we reflected upon both the way in which we approach leadership in a SF manner and the way in which we establish the 'credibility' and 'consistency' of our approach. Over six weeks of sessions within SLT meetings we took inspiration from James Kerr's *Legacy* (2013) and Simon Sinek's *Leaders Eat Last* (2014) to identify four key elements that would typify authentic leadership. Utilising the framework below we have set ourselves one single personalised action point upon which to focus. We used the frame to respond to four separate areas of reflection:

- Setting the culture

- Being visual

- Building true connections

- Leading humans not numbers

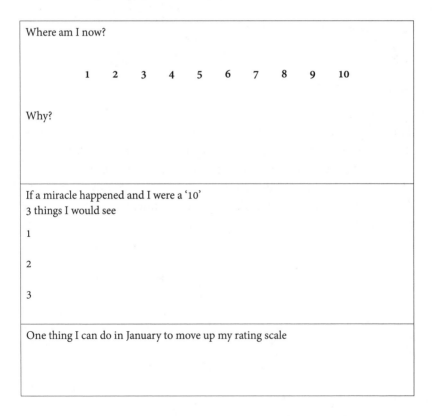

Where am I now?
1   2   3   4   5   6   7   8   9   10 Why?
If a miracle happened and I were a '10' 3 things I would see 1 2 3
One thing I can do in January to move up my rating scale

References

Birch, N. (2007) 'Picturing preferred futures: using case studies to investigate solution focused approaches to school improvement.' NCSL Research Associate Report, Nottingham.

Godat, D. (2013) 'Solution Focused Leadership – the other side of the elephant.' *InterAction*, November.

Hargreaves, D.H. (2010) *Creating a Self-Improving School System*. National College for Teaching and Leadership.

Jackson, P.Z. and McKergow, M. (2007) *The Solutions Focus*. Solutions Book Publications.

Kerr, J. (2013) *Legacy: What the All Blacks Can Teach Us About the Business of Life*. London: Constable.

Mahlberg, K. and Sjoblom, M. (2004) *Solution Focused Education*. Stockholm: Mareld.

McKergow, M. (2018) Personal communication with the Editor.

Röhrig, P. and Clarke, J. (eds) (2008) *57 SF Activities for Facilitators and Consultants: Putting Solutions Focus into Action*. Cheltenham: Solutions Books.

Shariff, A. and Abington, A. (2010) 'Solution focused strategy canvassing: an approach to enabling collective effort in making strategy happen.' *InterAction*, 2(1).

Sinek, S. (2014) *Leaders Eat Last: Why Some Teams Pull Together and Others Don't*. London: Portfolio.

Chapter 3

DIAGNOSES OR SOLUTIONS

Different Pathways for Supporting Students with Diverse Learning Needs

Kathleen Brown, PhD, Henri Pesonen, PhD and Tiina Itkonen, PhD

Disability diagnosis is required to obtain special education resources in most countries, including the US. This chapter explores an alternative to special education diagnosis, using the case of Finland, to examine the contrasting example of the US. This exploration is offered through the framework of Solutions Focused thinking within the area of educational assessment. A Solutions Focused approach to assessment empowers teachers to focus on providing the necessary adjustments to address the needs of students, rather than having to designate a label to access those resources. In this approach, there is little or no effort given toward the identification of disability or consideration of segregated classroom or separate school placements. The effort is spent toward looking for what works within the general education classroom.

Educational practices in Finland are unique in many ways. This uniqueness stems from a collaborative culture and professionalism which enables Solutions Focused thinking. The so-called 'culture of trust' (Sahlberg, 2007, p.156), on which education policy is grounded, awards teachers the authority and capacity to make most educational decisions (Pesonen *et al.*, 2015). This is possible because the teaching profession is well respected and highly sought. Teachers are exceedingly well trained compared to teachers in other parts of the world, and the selection process is arduous to become a teacher candidate in Finland. Approximately 10 per cent of applicants are accepted in the elementary school teacher education programme, 10–50 per cent to subject matter teacher education (depending on the subject), and approximately 3 per cent are selected to study special education at, for instance, the University of Helsinki (Finnish National Agency for Education, n.d.; Uusitalo-Malmivaara, personal communication, 2018). The teacher education plan of study involves five to six years of full-time instruction in the areas of child psychology, curriculum design, and assessment. In schools, therefore, no standardised testing is utilised to measure student performance, as teachers are the trusted professionals who know how and when to assess student learning for the purposes of informing teaching and learning. Further, teachers do not follow a curriculum as rigidly as in US schools. Finnish teachers have the latitude to create their own thematic units as long as they teach the grade-level content area goals of the broad national curriculum. Finnish teachers regularly work collaboratively to plan for and accomplish both.

In addition to a dynamic team process and teacher empowerment in instructional matters – including how to support students who demonstrate learning or behavioural difficulties – the immediate service provision for struggling students is possible because the concept of special needs is based on the term *difficulty* rather than *disability* for the majority of students (Itkonen and Jahnukainen, 2010). In the US, there are 13 discrete categories of disability which must be demonstrated through a multi-disciplinary team evaluation in order to qualify for special education services. Some students in Finland, primarily children with sensory, motor or developmental impairments, are described as having a disability. But most Finnish students who show delays in a broader array of learning and social/emotional contexts are considered to have a difficulty. The terms *difficulty* and *disability* denote a dramatic difference in the perception of permanence of the learning challenge. A difficulty is possibly a temporary challenge, while disability suggests a problem within the child that may not ever be resolved. Itkonen and Jahnukainen (2010) delineate Finnish categories of difficulties which encompass several of the indicators within the US definition of learning disabilities such as mathematics, linguistics, reading and writing. In addition, Finnish students who demonstrate challenges associated with social/emotional functioning are not considered as having emotional disabilities/disturbance but instead receive support in these areas.

The temporary status of children in Finland who require special education assistance is demonstrated in national numbers. In 2017, every sixth student received some form of support (either intensified or special) to supplement general education instruction. This translates to 17.5 per cent of Finnish students in grades 1–9 who receive either intensified support or have an Individual Education Plan (IEP) (Statistics Finland, 2018), and the number drops significantly in secondary schools (Hammerness *et al.*, 2017). In contrast, the US statistics show most students with disabilities are diagnosed later than their Finnish counterparts and remain in special education throughout their education (with the exception of students with speech and language impairments who are often declassified by age 12). The Finnish system, from education law down to practice, considers special education not as a 'place', but as a set of fluid strategies and supports which are designed at the school level based on child needs and collaborative decisions. There is no 'menu', in other words, from which to choose; each school team makes their own unique decisions based on the child's needs and input.

Hammerness *et al.* (2017) explain:

> Finnish education policy intentionally reflects an inclusive approach to children with special needs – in contrast to a more traditional approach which focuses on the 'disabilities' of children who must fit into the institutions who provide for them. (p.35)

The need *not* to classify or diagnose children stems from a broader philosophy in educational equity, which guides all education policy (Itkonen and Jahnukainen, 2007). For example, in international comparisons such as the Programme for International Student Achievement (PISA) exams, Finnish schools show the lowest between-school variation, and the youth's socio-economic status explains less than 5 per cent of the differences in PISA results across schools in the country. This means that it does not matter where a child attends school, and the child's parental background does not explain achievement. A clear contrast can be demonstrated in the US where achievement levels are closely aligned with socio-economic factors.

The following two cases examine the idea of Solutions Focused assessment as we see it in a Finnish context. In these scenarios, the school teams consider the problems presented as difficulties, not disabilities. The progression of service and supports by special education teachers is fluid.

CASE STUDY: **PAAVO**

Paavo is a nine-year-old third-grade student. He attends a suburban neighbourhood school of 200 students. Paavo likes school and has made many friends. He has found a passion in dancing and takes classes in a local dance school twice a week, which his parents have encouraged.

Although Paavo has many friends and excels in dancing, he has struggled in reading, writing and maths since first grade. Paavo's first-grade teacher almost immediately observed that Paavo had challenges in recognising letters and sounds. He received 'general support', which refers to the support that is provided in the general education classroom through differentiated activities (e.g. worksheets, small groups, rotations) and co-taught lessons (a special education teacher and the classroom teacher), and after-school club (staffed by trained Teacher Aides). The special education teacher, who screens all pupils in the beginning of first grade, also observed that Paavo was struggling.

Paavo's teacher paid close attention to Paavo's learning during the first months of school, and general support was considered insufficient. The teacher discussed his and the special education teacher's observations with the parents. He asked their permission to present Paavo's support needs to the student study team ('student welfare team' in Finnish), where teacher observations (logs, notes, maybe screening data) are shared. The purpose of the team was to discuss and decide if Paavo should receive intensified support. Intensified support refers to targeted pedagogical interventions for specific areas of learning, in which the student is struggling. In Paavo's case, intensified support meant weekly 1:1 lessons with the special education teacher for specific reading interventions both in and outside the regular classroom, which is mentioned in the intensified support plan documentation. Based on Paavo's wishes and the teachers' desire to provide highly motivating interventions, many of the reading topics were about dancing. The student study team also decided that it would be very important to support Paavo's self-esteem as he appeared to become self-conscious about his reading and scheduled regular meetings with the school counsellor.

Although it appeared that Paavo had made progress by the end of the second grade with additional support strategies added to his plan (text-to-speech tool and paraprofessional assigned to the classroom for half of the day), he continued to be behind in grade-level benchmarks in his reading, writing and maths skills. During the transition meeting to third grade, the new teacher felt that Paavo needed an individualised plan, but the second grade and special education teachers recommended waiting through the summer to see if Paavo matured. The team disagreed, but through collaborative talks decided to wait until the second or third month of the third grade to revisit the issue.

Now in third grade, Paavo still continues to struggle academically. His new teacher takes immediate action. The teacher meets with the student study team to discuss his concerns. It is decided that Paavo will receive more individualised supports, for example weekly 1:1 lessons with the special education teacher. No formal testing or diagnoses were needed to receive more individualised services. This does not mean that Paavo will study in a segregated or separate setting – he will still be in the same classroom with his peers with the most suitable supports. Individualised education means that learning goals are adjusted to meet present levels of performance or that some school subjects (e.g. foreign languages) are exempt. One might explain a Finnish IEP as a formal plan *for the teachers and other multi-disciplinary professionals* working with Paavo, on who will do what, how, when, and how to ensure that he is fully supported in all his learning and development.

CASE STUDY: **LIISA**

Liisa is a seven-year-old first-grader in Finland in a typical suburban neighbourhood school. She enjoys reading non-fiction books about different animals. Liisa has almost 20 different soft toy animals at home, which she has received over the years as birthday presents. Liisa was diagnosed with Autism Spectrum Disorder (ASD) at the age of two by a medical doctor when her parents became concerned about her lack of responsiveness in social situations. Since the diagnosis, she has presented some mild characteristics of ASD; for example, Liisa can be withdrawn in social situations (i.e. free play) when adult instruction or prompting are not present. Before first grade, she attended the Finnish compulsory preschool at the age of six, and daycare when she was five years old.

Presently, it is almost the end of the fall semester for Liisa as a first-grader. She has stated that she truly enjoys school. Although Liisa has an ASD diagnosis, she does not have an IEP nor has she attended lessons with a special education teacher. She is under general support, as diagnoses do not necessarily mean a child should have an IEP in schools in Finland. General support refers to education that is provided in general education classroom. She participates in joint classroom activities with other children and her learning has progressed very well. Specifically, Liisa's reading and maths skills appear to be outstanding as compared to her peers. Although she is continuing her academic success, the teacher has noticed that Liisa has some difficulties in unstructured social situations, particularly during recess. For example, the teacher observed that Liisa appears to be spending most of recess playtime alone. The teacher further observed that Liisa has a difficult time in writing tasks that require the use of a pencil (specifically, letter formation, pencil grip, spacing). Generating ideas and typing on the computer is not a problem, suggesting that pencil writing is a fine motor issue. The teacher further observed that other fine motor activities such as cutting can be challenging for Liisa.

To address the problems during recess, the teacher led a 'circle of friends' class meeting. She asked what each child did during recess (thus generating a list of possible activities such as swings, soccer, tag, hopscotch, field hockey). She then asked what could be done when a friend is alone and not playing with others. Through the process the class ended up with a recess buddy system where every child was assigned to a small group, and a simple process with which to decide what to play to ensure that all circle friends were included.

In order to support Liisa's writing and fine motor development, the teacher discussed her observations with the parents and colleagues. She asked their permission to present Liisa's support needs in student welfare group so that Liisa can receive intensified support as soon as possible. The student welfare group members are typically classroom teachers (who have concerns with regard to certain students), special education teacher, principal, school psychologist, school counsellor and school nurse. Intensified support consists of targeted interventions for specific skills with which the student is experiencing difficulties. Liisa's teacher recommended that the lessons be planned in collaboration with the special education teacher, and both teachers should be working in the same classroom frequently to support Liisa's fine motor activities (and use the adult presence to support other students as well). The teacher and the student welfare group also recommended that Liisa always have access to a laptop or tablet computer, as well as practise fine motor skills with the special education teacher. Ongoing observation of the overall social skills and fine motor development will continue to ensure that Liisa receives more individualised support right away, if needed, so that she will not fall behind in school.

These case studies illustrate the concept of Solutions Focused assessment in Finland. One component of this is the use of authentic assessment by the Finnish teachers who watch the academic and social development of the children carefully and use these observations to inform instructional decisions. To fully understand this concept, it is helpful to unpack these cases through a comparison to US special education assessment.

Curriculum-based measurements

The term 'curriculum-based measurements' (CBM) is widely used around the world but it can be operationalised quite differently in national contexts and the data derived from these assessments can prove to be especially dissimilar. In the US, it is commonplace to purchase web-based tools which standardise brief assessments given regularly and used to identify students who are falling behind. There are reports available to aggregate or disaggregate the outcomes of these content or skill-based achievement samples. The web-based reports can be presented in tables or graphs which show visual comparisons of achievement levels of targeted learners and their peers.

Finnish teachers collect data but there is no formal mechanism to present graphs or formal data regarding students who may be falling behind to the team. The observations and CBMs are directly related to instruction. In this regard, assessment is closely aligned with instruction and the constructs assessed are exactly related to the skills embedded in the lessons. As such, it can be said that overall CBM in Finland is a highly valid and reliable assessment. For both Liisa and Paavo, the teachers were able to observe and write notes and logs as they saw a need for notation. The reports can be informal or non-existent.

In Finland, teachers can customise assessments for individuals to create the best possible, more motivating situation. In the case of Liisa, the teacher would use stories or passages about animals to support Liisa's preference and interests. Similarly, Paavo's reading materials focused around dance to increase motivation by using his favorite topic for supplemental instruction and assessment. Teachers can create opportunities to capitalise on student strengths to assess growth. In this way, in Finland the CBM increases the reliability of the achievement outcomes since the student is happily engaged in the activity. For students like Liisa with fine motor difficulty, the teacher might use stuffed animals for maths screening to eliminate the fine motor component from the assessment. In the case of Paavo, the teachers included his interests and strengths in the area of dance as an integral part of the assessment and instructional planning. This aligns well with a central tenet of Solutions Focused assessment, which is that it intentionally seeks to create the best possible setting and conditions to encourage the child's strengths to emerge.

It is important to listen to the preferences and/or desires of the children themselves. Solutions Focused assessment, which considers the child's voice, is an essential aspect of authentic evaluation. Finnish education law (Basic Education Act [642/2010] Finnish Ministry of Culture and Education) in fact *requires involvement of the pupil* in the assessment and instructional planning process. The child is also asked to specify in which areas he/she faces challenges and needs additional help. In Solutions Focused thinking it is clear that the pupil's point of view is tantamount in the understanding of the problem and the solutions-finding process. Sahlberg (2018) describes this requirement in Finland as a way to move forward:

> Empower your students by involving the assessing and reflecting on their own learning and then incorporate that information into collective human judgement about teaching and learning (supported by national big data). Because there are different ways students can be smart in schools, no one way of measuring student achievement will reveal success. Students' voices about their own ideas and growth may provide those tiny clues that can uncover important trends for improving learning. (p.43)

The goal of CBM and observations in Finland is to discover the better or best way to teach the student. The school team is never concerned with diagnosis or labels in these observations. All assessment is an information-seeking effort and is continuous through daily classroom events. In Finland, teachers aren't interested in labelling the difficulty as Learning Disability since the label is vague and meaningless for solutions-finding assessments. The guiding question for teachers is focused on how to reach a child by listening carefully for the tiny clues that can unlock potential.

In the case of Liisa, the diagnosis of ASD was obtained by the physician. The teachers conducted their own assessments based on her learning and social needs. The information contained in the medical report has little bearing on the educational supports and interventions. Teachers provided instructional, social and emotional scaffolds as they perceived them. It is possible a student would have a medical diagnosis without any educational supports. However, it *might* be that in Liisa's case, the outside diagnosis prompted the teacher to observe recess, as some students with ASD might demonstrate social difficulties. However, a student with a medically diagnosed social communication disorder might not receive school-based supports if diagnosis does not affect student learning.

More formal assessments can however be used in some situations in Finland. Specifically, during the fall semester of first and second grades, special education teachers screen student reading, writing and comprehension skills, as well as maths skills of all students. Students are also screened during the fourth and sixth grades before the end of the school year. Special education teachers use published and research-based assessment and screening materials. Other times, special education teachers can assess reading and other content achievement skills if the information is considered vital in order to support the student. In these instances, after consultation with the classroom teacher, the special education teacher also uses published assessments or screening materials which are research-based. This is always the decision of the teachers and is not obligatory. Parents would be consulted and informed, but no formal, legal permission would be required, as the teachers are trusted in their professional judgement. In addition, for instance, physical therapists might have regular assessments on the student's physical development and this is attached to the IEP documentation.

A change in the US identification process for students with suspected disabilities allows for early intervention services in a three-tiered process called response to intervention (RtI). In this structure, teachers use CBM data to demonstrate a learning problem by tracking achievement scores on short and regularly administered probes. Students who do not demonstrate improvement are pulled into small-group instruction typically for a few hours per week where additional CBM probes are administered and charted over time. As explicitly stated in the Individuals with Disabilities Education Act (IDEA, 2004) the purpose of this early intervention process is to gather evidence to show that the unexplained underachievement is not caused by inadequate instruction. As such, this latest iteration of US federal special education law asks educators to consider if the problem can be attributed to the instruction rather than an intrinsic malady within the child. However, the supposition remains that RtI begins only when disability is suspected. To receive supports through special education, though, a child must be evaluated as specified in IDEA, and qualify under one of the 13 eligibility categories. Although RtI is not specifically mandated by the law, IDEA allocated 10 per cent of special education funds to be available for evidence-based interventions prior to, and as a part of, special education evaluation. In order to receive services, the schools must follow the referral and identification process, which results in both a label and an IEP. The impetus for RtI was to design an approach to intervene early and avoid a special education label and the discrepancy model for eligibility, which Fuchs *et al.* (2003) and others described as a 'wait to fail' model. Since the passage of IDEA 2004, the US has seen a slight decrease in the number of students identified with Specific Learning Disabilities, while the percentage (approximately 13%) of US students who are classified as children with disabilities remains consistent overall (U.S. Department of Education, National Center for Education Statistics, 2016). Critics of the RtI process complain that it extends the time requirements to complete an evaluation and can result in long delays before a decision to diagnose and develop an IEP (Hudson and McKenzie, 2016).

General education classroom interventions and supports

Finnish teachers are considered experts in content and pedagogy. In scenarios like the cases of Liisa and Paavo, the general classroom teacher is the first to look for new ways to reach the children. In this way, Solutions Focused thinking is employed from the earliest stages of assessment and instruction. As noted, special education supports are fluid. The teacher can request a paraprofessional or a special education teacher when the general classroom teacher decides it would be beneficial. Decisions are made through an 'in-house' collaborative process.

Paraprofessionals in Finland are not usually assigned to specific classrooms. The decisions regarding the work of paraprofessionals is collaborative. Similarly, with special education teachers, paraprofessionals might be asked to teach a lesson to the large group while the classroom teacher works with individual children. The roles of the adults are flexible and can be changed to support individual students and groups as needed.

There is an exception to this in Finland where personal assistants can be assigned to a particular child, typically a child with a significant disability who may require support in self-management activities.

Hammerness *et al.* (2017) discuss what could be described as Solutions Focused thinking by teachers:

> Teachers are constantly rearranging student groups, identifying children who need help, paying special attention to the student who has questions or misunderstands, to the student whose attention lags, as well as if there are more considerable challenges with comprehension, analysis, or understanding. (p.37)

For more persistent challenges, teams are formed to include school-based as well as community-based members. Within the school, welfare group members are typically classroom teachers (who have concerns with regard to certain students), special education teacher, principal, school psychologist, school counsellor and school nurse. As needed, social workers from health services, representatives from health and mental health community, or from public housing, may join the team. These outside professionals expand the reach of the school team to assess needs and offer relevant supports which focus on the whole child.

Individual Education Plans are developed in Finland, but they are not highly legalised documents (Neal and Kirp, 1985) or grounded on an over-abundance of rules (Kirp and Jensen, 1986). Rather, the IEP is a way to organise a plan which states who, what, when and how supports will be given. Perhaps this difference stems from the origins of special education in these two countries, and subsequent conceptualisations. In the US, the law emerged as a result of court cases and provides detailed due process provisions, including a process for litigation. In Finland, special education emerged from educators and the system is based on trust and students' perceived educational needs. This difference enables in-house, teacher-based decisions in Finland without the concern of legal action from opponents.

Educational leaders in Finland

Terano *et al.* (2011) considered Finland to be a shining example of the best practices and conditions in their international comparison of multiple factors affecting inclusive education:

The cases of Finland focus on the ways in which high quality teachers have been developed through making the teaching profession attractive and setting high standards. These are enabled by generous levels of public investment and a genuine commitment to high quality and inclusive education, as well as developing an awareness that education is a shared responsibility amongst all the members of a society. (p.viii)

The collaborative structure of teacher work allows teachers to share ideas and materials, and seek support from one another. The principals do meet with their teachers, but the purpose is not to evaluate the teacher, but to have a professional development discussion of the areas in which the teacher feels s/he is strong, and areas where s/he feels could grow. The discussion then evolves to possible ways to move toward that growth. Also, the principals are instructional leaders. Often at the elementary level, the principal may even be scheduled to teach a particular subject of their own speciality – for example, geography to a fifth-grade class on Tuesdays.

Disability labels in schools

Although many developed countries espouse a social model of disability, in reality the medical model dominates the practice where the process of 'labelling' is a necessary component to access special education resources. A disability label can offer some benefits in understanding the challenges presented; however, the tendency for the child to be described by the label diminishes attention to other aspects of their personality or strengths (VanSwet et al., 2011). In essence the child can become the label. Finland is an exception to this practice as the medical diagnosis isn't necessarily important information when considering special educational needs. Finnish schools support students using fluid and flexible systems that enable just-in-time help without the need to label students at all.

The ability to offer help without label avoids a bevy of problems associated with the construct of disability for what might be very temporary challenges. Disability labels can be tied to lowered expectations or self-fulfilling prophecy for the individuals themselves. For US teachers, the term can lead to the belief that general classroom teachers are not qualified to teach the student and this can create increased push for additional resources. As well, the drive toward segregated instructional settings is strengthened by the 'othering' associated with the term *disability*. By using the term *support needs* for struggling students, the

Finnish schools can capitalise on early intervention research findings without the myriad of these negative effects. In fact, 50 per cent of all students by the end of their compulsory education (ninth grade) have received some form of support by special education teachers or supports services, maybe not even realising it themselves (Sahlberg, 2011).

Skrtic (2003) described overrepresentation of some US ethnic minority students in special education as an unintended consequence of organisations who are unable to adapt when faced with increasing diversity. His perspective examined the US tendency to establish structures in public schools that served to segregate students who are different rather than adapt to the changing demographic. The assessment of suspected disabilities in US schools, even within the structure of RtI early intervention, attests to an antiquated paradigm. Labelling a suspected difference as an impairment enables the organisation to remove students who are challenging. The organisation can justify the status quo if the difficulties can be attributed to disability. This approach disregards the idea that the challenges might be temporary and resolved with access to high-quality early intervention.

The idea of Solutions Focused assessment allows us to understand the aspects of very effective practices used in Finland to reconsider assessment for special education as a model for other countries. This revised view of support structures can serve to empower teachers to be creative and collaborative without the constraints of traditional special education assessment for the purpose of label identification. Solutions Focused assessment can enhance the ability of an organisation to adapt to diverse needs and challenges in an ever-changing environment.

Conclusion

This chapter demonstrates an example of Solutions Focused assessment in special education. We offer the example of Finland as an alternative to a bureaucratic and diagnostic identification process to access special education. From the earliest stages of assessment and instruction to special education supports, which are fluid without the need of any official diagnosis of students, Finnish practices prove higher achievement outcomes overall. The unique context of Finland illustrates the conditions under which such an alternative is possible. Finnish cultural underpinnings support teachers to make collaborative instructional decisions at the best possible time in the child's development without the yoke of procedural requirements or documented evidence to prove additional support is needed. The shared national goal of equity and trust in teachers empowers the entire system to shift focus toward what helps a child's development rather than what might be a disability.

Although the intent of the RtI initiative in the US was to provide individualised support to children regardless of the type and degree of their disability, the unintended consequence was a bureaucratisation of learning and individual needs. For example, in the law, US schools have 60 days to perform the evaluation of a child from the day of parental consent, and special education services cannot be provided until the child is found eligible and the parent consents to services and educational placement. That amounts to two months of a school year. Solutions Focused teacher(s) would have tried a host of strategies, collaborated to gather ideas, asked the child for input, and pulled in resources for the classroom teacher to act immediately to support the child.

Perhaps a Solutions Focused way of thinking about children is slowly coming to all school systems, as society's understanding of *typical* and *atypical* is changing. Increased demographic diversity about multi-culturalism, sexual orientation and multiple intelligences, along with advances in technology ('universal design') allows us to be more inclusive in society and find new ways to respond to various needs.

In this chapter we propose the use of Solutions Focused assessment in special education as a better process for evaluating and responding to the learning difficulties that are inevitable and apparent in schools all over the world. The contrast of these two countries demonstrate a distinct difference in the policy and cultural norms manifested in the treatment of children. At the heart of this difference is the capacity of an organisation to shift focus from what is inherently wrong with a child to what is inherently wrong with the instruction. We opine that in order to achieve this shift of focus, we must begin with the assumption that all teachers can develop the skills to support students who are struggling when a fluid and flexible structure is available. Solutions Focused assessment is an integral component to this possibility. We have used Finland as a case study to illustrate aspects of Solutions Focused thinking, such as strength-based assessments and supports, teacher-led information gathering, child input, collaborative problem solving, and ongoing review. These aspects ensure a fluid set of educational supports without the need for an official disability diagnosis. The negative impact and unintended consequences of an unnecessary disability label as the only means of access to support has the effect of limiting the growth of the organisation. The fundamental idea here is that categorical eligibilities assign the blame of learning (or the lack thereof) to the child. Solutions Focused education assigns the burden to the school system by targeting what supports to provide, how, by whom, and when.

Policymakers can enable this systems-change through a revision in resource allocation which promotes flexibility in access to special education resources when and where they are needed. Teachers can be elevated in their practice through training and empowerment to make decisions about resources. Collaboration builds trust when time is available for the hard work involved in developing strong and effective teams who can focus attention on creative curricular solutions. We believe this can occur anywhere.

References

Basic Education Act (642/2010) Finnish Ministry of Culture and Education. Basic Education Act Amendment (2010) Finnish National Board of Education. Available at www.oph.fi/download/132551_amendments_and_additions_to_national_core_curriculum_basic_education.pdf (accessed 22/10/2018).

Burnett, N. and Brown, K. (2013) *Solutions Focused Special Education Assessment* [White paper]. Available at http://solution-support.co.uk/wp-content/uploads/2013/03/Solution-Focused-Special-Education.pdf (accessed 22/10/2018).

Finnish National Agency for Education (n.d.) *Finnish Education in a Nutshell.* Available at www.oph.fi/download/146428_Finnish_Education_in_a_Nutshell.pdf (accessed 22/10/2018).

Fuchs, D., Mock, D., Morgan, P. and Young, C. (2003) 'Responsiveness to intervention: definitions, evidence, and implications for the learning disabilities construct.' *Learning Disabilities Research and Practice*, 18, 157–171.

Hammerness, K., Ahtiainen, R. and Sahlberg, P. (2017) *Empowered Educators in Finland: How High-Performing Systems Shape Teaching Quality*. San Francisco, CA: Jossey-Bass.

Hudson, T.M. and McKenzie, R.G. (2016) 'The impact of RTI on timely identification of students with Specific Learning Disabilities.' *Learning Disabilities: A Multidisciplinary Journal*, 21(2), 46–58. Available at http://summit.csuci.edu:2048/login?url=http://search.ebscohost.com/login.aspx?direct=true&db=eric&AN=EJ1168882&site=ehost-live (accessed 22/10/2018).

Individuals With Disabilities Education Act, 20 U.S.C. § 1400 (2004).

Itkonen, T. and Jahnukainen, M. (2007) 'An analysis of accountability policies in Finland and the United States.' *International Journal of Disability, Development and Education*, 54(1), 5–23.

Itkonen, T. and Jahnukainen, M. (2010) 'Disability or learning difficulty? Politicians or educators? Constructing special education in Finland and the United States.' *Comparative Sociology*, 9, 182–201. Doi: 10.1163/156913210X12536181351033.

Jahnukainen, M. and Itkonen, T. (2016) 'Tiered intervention: history and trends in Finland and the United States.' *European Journal of Special Needs Education,* 31(3), 140–150.

Kirp, D.L. and Jensen, D. (1986) (eds) *School Days, Rule Days: The Legislation and Regulation in Education*. Philadelphia, PA: Falmer Press.

Neal. D. and Kirp, D.L. (1985) 'The allure of legalization reconsidered: the case of special education.' *Law and Contemporary Problems*, 48(1), 63–87.

Pesonen, H., Itkonen, T., Jahnukainen, M., Kontu, E., Kokko, T., Ojala, T. and Pirttimaa, R. (2015) 'The implementation of new special education legislation in Finland.' *Educational Policy*, 29(1), 162–178. Doi: 10.1177/0895904814556754.

Sahlberg, P. (2018) *FinnishED Leadership: Four Big, Inexpensive Ideas to Transform Education*. Thousand Oaks, CA: Corwin.

Sahlberg, P. (2007) 'Education policies for raising student learning: the Finnish approach.' *Journal of Education Policy*, 22(2), 147–171. Doi:10.1080/02680930601158919.

Sahlberg, P. (2011) *Finnish Lessons: What Can the World Learn From Educational Change in Finland?* New York: Teachers College Press.

Skrtic, T. (2003) 'An organizational analysis of the overrepresentation of poor and minority students in special education.' *Multiple Voices for Ethnically Diverse Exceptional Learners*, 6(1), 41–57.

Statistics Finland (2018) *Increasingly more comprehensive school pupils received intensified or special support*. Available at www.stat.fi/til/erop/2017/erop_2017_2018-06-11_tie_001_en.html (accessed 22/10/2018).

Terano, M., Slee, R., Scott, D., Husbands, C., Naoum, D., Zotzmann, K. and Kingdon, G. (2011) *International Productive Practices in Education. (A Research Report)*. New Delhi: Save the Children.

U.S. Department of Education, National Center for Education Statistics (2016) *Children and youth with disabilities*. Available at https://nces.ed.gov/programs/coe/indicator_cgg.asp (accessed 22/10/2018).

Uusitalo-Malmivaara, L. (2018) Personal communication. 16 January 2018.

VanSwet, J., Wichers-Bot, J. and Brown, K. (2011) 'Solution focused assessment: rethinking labels to support inclusive education.' *International Journal of Inclusive Education*, 1–15. Doi:10.1080/13603110903456615.

Chapter 4

SOLUTIONS FOCUSED SPECIAL EDUCATION HUMAN RESOURCES

Nick Burnett and Drew Allison

Introduction

The focus of this chapter is to explore a Solutions Focused (SF) approach to the human resources aspect of Solutions Focused Special Education (SFSE), which is also largely relevant to any education setting.

The chapter starts with an exploration of the importance of culture in developing and supporting SFSE approaches.[1]

The chapter then explores the more practical aspects around human resources including recruitment, retention, professional learning, support for staff, performance management and debriefing, with practical examples shared throughout.

Culture and conversations

Schools already have some staff members who, often without knowing, will be highly SF. Others will be keen to identify, analyse and solve problems.

It is clear that becoming a SF staff can involve a subtle but significant culture shift for at least some of the staff members. But where does a school's culture come from, and how might it be changed?

Culture is basically 'the way we do things around here'. And the way we do things is continually constructed and reconstructed in the (everyday) conversations of those involved. In our formal and informal

---

1   We'd like to thank Ivan Webb for sharing his thoughts on this element.

conversations we continually construct (and reconstruct) our knowledge, actions, arrangements, relationships and tools. Each conversation occurs in a context that involves the histories, hopes and interests of those involved (staff, students, families, the school, communities) as well as policies, regulations and resources.

That is, the culture emerges, continues and/or changes from conversations; therefore changing the culture means changing the conversations.

In schools, 'conversations' occur at a range of levels including individual reflections, chats, meetings, workshops, publications and reporting. Conversations are central to formal processes such as staff selection, performance management and staff support (coaching, mentoring and debriefing). At the same time, the school's structure, organisation, and associated staff roles, enable and/or constrain the conversations that occur.

Ideally the whole organisation and operation of the school will be SF. This will provide staff with the experience of being the beneficiaries of such an approach and so confirm the validity of adopting a SF approach in areas beyond education.

We will now explore the topic of recruitment which is obviously important in any education setting but has particular relevance to the special education sector as in many parts of the world this is often the sector facing the most significant challenges to recruitment.

Recruitment

It is suggested that from the very first interaction with prospective staff, taking a SF approach is beneficial. How staff are recruited varies widely from one system to another and so advertising for staff may not be directly in the school's control. Even when this is the case, the school publications can give a very strong message to prospective employees that the school is adopting a SF approach. Reviewing all publications through a SF lens is an important role for leadership staff to undertake. Probably even more important is leadership staff 'walking the talk' in a SF way.

As stated earlier, it is through the ongoing conversations that the culture is enacted. Having a good fit between policy and practice helps reinforce the school's desire to adopt a SF approach. Within special education one of the key elements to this will be the way students are viewed and talked about and there is more on this in Chapter 5 on teaching and learning.

The final aspect in relation to recruitment is in the interviewing process. It is suggested that adopting a SF approach to interviewing again helps reinforce the culture of the school from the very outset.

Below is a case study from one of the authors, sharing the challenges and solutions they implemented within their school in relation to recruitment. It should be noted that this is from a mainstream school but as was noted in the opening to the chapter, many, if not all, of the approaches shared will be equally relevant to any school setting.

CASE STUDY: **SF APPROACH TO SCHOOL STAFF RECRUITMENT**

A redesign of the schooling model within the local authority led to the change of the student age bracket that the school catered for. This led to:

- forced redeployment of staff within the system

- retirement and resignation of experienced and valued staff

- a move to a new site and building

- doubling of student intake within very short period of time, resulting in a need to more than double the number of school staff

- a high number of applications for vacant positions which used 'standard' templates – this also extended to the provision of references; both made it extremely hard to identify quality

- vacant positions predominantly being filled with staff who were inexperienced, 'forcibly' working in a school not of their choosing or from overseas recruitment agencies

- a high staff turnover, with some staff staying at the school for only one term.

All of the above had a significant impact on the students. Their best interests were not being served and outcomes, by any measure, were significantly impacted as students were not being provided with the consistency, routine and high-quality learning opportunities to which they were entitled.

This necessitated a change to how the school had traditionally recruited so that high-quality candidates could be attracted, employed and retained.

The solutions
Identifying the recruitment Future Perfect

1. This was co-developed between the school leadership team, governors, staff, local education authority and local universities. All were engaged as appropriate to identify the preferred staffing model to meet the school's vision and to completely redesign the recruitment process.

   The school had successfully employed some high-quality staff. These were engaged to identify what attracted them to the school, its strengths and what made them remain committed to enjoying their work. This shift from a focus on the problem to identifying solutions was a major enabler in the process that followed to recruit and maintain a capable, committed and dynamic workforce.

2. A strategic decision was taken to attract staff not only by the advertised role but also by making the recruitment process innovative and engaging. The selection process focused on what candidates can do and are capable of rather than a deficit model.

3. Money was committed to the process for prominent advertising locally and nationally, development of recruitment resources and training of selection panel members (staff and students).

4. An application pack for candidates was developed which included:

   › clearly defined role description

   › key selection criteria explicitly tied to advertised role

   › explicit expectations/KPIs

> key data on school/community and strategic plan

> professionally produced 'virtual' walkthrough of school

> checklist of how to apply for and be successful in getting the role:

  – what to focus on and include in the letter

  – what to include in CV

  – electronic application form

  – expectations/protocols regarding contacting the school prior to application/interview

> outline of interview process:

  – full day

  – group tour

  – teach 20-minute lesson (focus, group size, observers and observation criteria explicitly shared)

  – interview by student panel (focus of interview explicitly highlighted)

  – formal panel interview (panel members and key focus shared)

  – timeline and process for contacting successful and unsuccessful applicants.

5. There was an explicit committment to staff professional development that would prepare them for promotion (internally or externally) within a two to three-year period. Commitment to this professional development was also an explicit expectation.

The successful implementation of the recruitment processes had the following benefits and impact:

• Longlisting/shortlisting became more efficient as applications that did not explicitly address the criteria and follow the process could be excluded, resulting in highly capable and competitive 'fields'.

- At interview candidates were fully able to highlight their strengths and capabilities:

  › They were fully aware of the specifics of the role and able to showcase their strengths.

  › A more balanced view of the candidate was achieved as they could be assessed over the period of the day interacting with students in the teaching and interview components and with staff in observations, tours and formal interviews.

  › Candidates could formulate specific questions relating to the role.

  › Candidates could better form a view about whether the school was a match for their capabilities. The final interview question for all candidates was always 'If offered this position, are you still a firm candidate and are you able to adhere to the commitments that you have made throughout the process?'

Key outcomes from implementation of the approach

In the previous two-year period, over 70 per cent of new appointments left the school within one year of appointment (this was significant as the number of staff had more than doubled). After a period of four years, staff turnover reduced dramatically to 15 per cent and subsequently less.

In addition, with the reduction in turnover of staffing, student attendance, attainment and behaviour improved. External monitoring highlighted the stabilisation of the workforce and the quality of the teaching and support as significant factors in improving student attainment, behaviour and attendance. There was also improvement in staff satisfaction and wellbeing indicators, as well as spending on recruitment being reduced significantly once the process was embedded.

Final comments

Within education, recruitment has traditionally been formulaic and compliance focused which can detract from the core purpose of employing high-quality staff to meet the needs of the students and facilitate the delivery of the school's strategic intent. The approach outlined above met the obligatory requirements whilst explicitly addressing the preferred future through enabling candidates to highlight their talents at all phases of the process.

Retention

Whilst recruitment is obviously a key aspect to HR in SFSE, retaining staff is as important. Under the heading of retention, we have included organisation of staffing and ongoing support and performance management.

There are high numbers of beginning teachers leaving, or in many cases never entering the teaching profession. Also, there continues to be many issues around the ongoing support to staff in special education, with higher levels of injury and sickness than in other sectors. Therefore, the topic of retention is a crucial aspect of SFSE human resources.

Organisation

As was identified earlier, culture is the way we do things round here and the organisation of the school has a big influence on this. Whilst virtually all schools are likely to have some sort of hierarchical leadership and management structure, how inclusive and democratically they operate gives some clear messages. What teams are set up and who is on them? Within SFSE what roles do teaching assistants and paraprofessionals play within the school and in relation to which students?

Within a SFSE school it is suggested that the decision-making structures and processes will be very open and democratic to enable the conversations identified as being so important to take place. In addition, the opportunities for support will be available for all staff members.

Adopting a SF structure shapes and clarifies how meetings are run and what protocols are used, and this enables confidence that everyone has a say within a SF framework.

Professional learning

The opportunity for all staff to access professional learning is a key element in both the retention and the performance of staff in SFSE.

We will now explore a range of opportunities and structures in which SFSE professional learning may operate.

Meetings

Unfortunately, the experience of many of the readers of this book may well be that they do not see any benefit in the many meetings they attend and that in fact these aren't professional learning opportunities. We accept that there needs to be a place for the passing on of information and for discussion but analysing the best communication method to achieve the most productive use of precious time is a key leadership skill.

The range of possible meetings is significant but below is a brief suggestion about a SF approach to the structure of meetings. Many more ideas about how to infuse a SF approach are available in *57 SF Activities for Facilitators and Consultants: Putting Solutions Focus into Action* (Röhrig and Clarke, 2008).

Suggested SF meeting structure

- Share two or more 'sparkling moments' from the day/week so far with colleagues.

- Depending on the topic under discussion/consideration, use scaling to explore what's currently going well.

- Explore what could take the scoring one point higher.

- Share small next steps.

In earlier chapters it was mentioned that there are a range of ways of adopting a SF approach to meetings dependent on content and we would encourage you to explore these further for ideas.

Self-Managed Learning

Self-Managed Learning (SML) is increasingly used in training and development. It has the benefit of closely integrating individual and organisational goals, practical application and reflection, individual and shared responsibility. In a SFSE environment it is suggested that there would be multi-professional membership on each of the learning teams to encourage wider participation and suggestion making.

A key element in successful SML is the effective functioning of the 'learning-team'. Effective teams create a true 'learning environment' in which individuals can reflect on their learning and develop their practice.

Responsibility for action remains with the individual but they are able to rehearse and reflect within the learning team in addition to getting practical input and sharing ideas. The needs and priorities of individuals are usually detailed in a 'learning contract'. Part of the role of the learning team is to support and challenge individuals in the implementation of their contract. This focus on the specific helps to ensure that sustainable change takes place.

Typically, team meetings are divided into individual timeslots. Prior to the meeting, members decide how they wish to make use of their timeslot. They may choose to present some information, lead a discussion, ask for ideas and input, share difficulties and challenges, or anything else, provided it is directed towards helping them to fulfil their learning contract. During these timeslots the full attention of team members is focused on the particular circumstances and needs of one of their number. After the meeting, team members then reflect on the input and insights from the meeting and how they can use them to assist in implementing their learning contract.

Usually learning-teams meet every four to eight weeks over a period of months. Having an agreed SF process for running the learning-team meetings can be highly beneficial and help members of the team stay on track with keeping the focus on the 'customer' with the area of practice they wish to discuss. Harry Norman has developed a useful 'Solutions Focused Reflecting' (SFR) team approach with Michael Hjerth and Tim Pidsley (2005).

Initially participants may feel constrained by the discipline of the SFR team format. However, they adapt to the structure, and find that the boundaries and time constraints actually work to their advantage.

SFR teams operate in a resource focused way even if the team members have no pre-existing SF skills. The SFR team format is an analogue of a SF Coaching process – a cycle of *preparing, presenting, clarifying, affirming, reflecting and closing,* detailed in Table 4.1.

Table 4.1: SF reflecting team structure

PAUSE	ACTIVITIES	LISTENING & SPEAKING RULES
Preparing	Each person who hopes to receive help prepares for the meeting and is clear about what they hope to gain from the meeting.	
Presenting	Team members take it in turns to receive help. The costumer for receiving help describes the situation they would like some help with.	Only the costumer spaeks. When there is written preparation the costumer may elect to have another team member read the preparation out loud.
Clarifying	The team is interested in clarifying the story so far and interested in the costumers skills, abilities, resources and achievements. Questions for clarification are encouraged - e.g. 'What?', When?'. 'Where?', 'Who?' and 'How?' based questions. 'Why?' questions and closed questions are discouraged. It is not necessary for team members to ask questions that build a theme or thread.	Team members each take a turn to ask one question and one follow-up question, and then remain silent until their turn comes around again.
Affirming	The team members tell the costumer briefly what impresses each of them most about him, or her, in the situation they have described. Team members may offer similar compliments.	The team members speak in any order. The costumer remains silent.
Reflecting	Each team member says one thing at a time or 'passes'. Sometimes team members offer reflections triggered by previous reflections. The team continues until everyone has said all they want to say, or time runs out.	The team members speak in sequence. The costumer remains silent. (If the team's reflections are clearly and persistently based on a misunderstanding the costumer may speak very briefly to point this out.)
Closing	The costumer responds briefly to what was said in the reflecting phase, usually stating what seems most applicable and specifies some course of action.	Only the costumer speaks.

Source: Norman, Pidsley and Hjerth (2005)

SFR teams usually have between five and eight members. Each team member taking a 'turn' receives help for a maximum of half an hour. Thus a team session for five members, each taking a turn, needs two and a half hours and therefore may be split over a number of meetings. It is suggested that when planning a half-hour turn, the timing of the phases should be something like this:

- presenting – four minutes
- clarifying – ten minutes
- affirming – two minutes
- reflecting – ten minutes
- closing – four minutes.

Coaching and mentoring

One of the authors has some developing work in the leadership conversational space called 'The Myriad of Leadership Conversations' (Burnett, 2017).

In this work it is suggested that 1:1 colleague conversations will largely operate in three positions:

- supervisor
- mentoring
- coaching.

As shown in Figure 4.1, '1:1 colleague conversational positions', which conversational position is taken will be dependent on both context and staff member.

For example: in a high-risk situation then telling is more likely to be useful (mentoring and coaching as a reflection approach can be highly useful); a beginning teacher is more likely to benefit from mentoring (combination of asking and telling), whereas an experienced teacher is more likely to benefit from coaching.

What is suggested is that each of the conversations undertaken by leaders has a continuum of 'conversational positions' which are *highly dependent on context and the individual with whom the leader is having the conversation.*

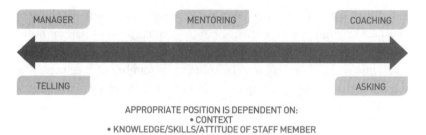

Figure 4.1: 1:1 colleague conversational positions
(Workplace Conversation Continuum)
Source: Burnett (2017)

The focus of this section of the chapter is on the coaching and mentoring spaces that could be either informally or formally set up within SFSE. Whilst the focus of the Myriad of Leadership Conversations is clearly on leaders' conversations, it is suggested that it is highly beneficial for professional learning that all staff within a SFSE environment learn and use these skills. We will move to the supervisor conversational position when performance management (or, as we would recommend, 'Performance Development') is explored, before moving on to the support aspect of SFSE human resources.

Coaching

We are deliberately starting with the coaching conversational position. We believe that it is good practice for staff to start their interactions by asking themselves the question: 'Is this a coaching opportunity?' This could be either by asking the person 'Would you like me to coach you on this?' or by asking themselves whether this is an opportunity to coach this person. The rationale for this is that generally we are ATMs (Automatic Telling Machines!). Whilst well intentioned, and appropriate on some occasions, it does mean there is a missed opportunity to help the other person help themselves.

The purpose of the coaching should always be about growth and development for the person. As was identified in an online course run by Richard Boyatzis and colleagues at Case Western University on coaching, an important aspect to consider is: 'Are we coaching with compassion or for compliance?' If it is about compliance, and sometimes it is, then we would argue it's not a coaching conversation.

In the coaching conversational position, there is a continuum of approaches that may be implemented within the organisation. As identified in Figure 4.2, 'The Workplace Coaching Continuum', these range from formal coaching, which is planned at agreed times and is largely coachee driven, to 'water-cooler' coaching, or what some call 'corridor coaching', where there are short coaching-style interactions to check on progress or as a response to something that emerges. These may be coachee led, leader or colleague led or a combination of both. The final approach is that of 'coaching approach' to conversations. This can be best summarised as interactions that are leader led but where they use more questions than answers alongside listening more than talking; these can be implemented in many contexts.

Another way of viewing these coaching interactions is along the formal–informal continuum, where the formal is the planned coaching interactions and the informal is the coaching approach.

Figure 4.2: The Workplace Coaching Continuum
Source: Burnett (2017)

As identified in the 1:1 colleague conversational positions in Figure 4.1, what these look and sound like will vary according to the context and the person in conversation with the leader.

The *formal* coaching aspect is as near to 'pure coaching' as is possible in a work situation. Pure coaching could be defined as:

> A one-to-one conversation focused on the enhancement of learning and development through increasing self-awareness and a sense of personal responsibility where the coach facilitates the self-directed learning of the coachee through questioning, active listening and appropriate challenge in a supportive and encouraging climate. (Van Nieuwerburgh 2016, p.508)

This is mainly coachee led with the focus being on their learning and development, coaching with compassion, as opposed to being about completing a task that is required by the leader or colleague.

The *informal* end of the continuum is very much in the 'coaching approach' to conversations space where the person is:

- asking questions

- listening to connect

- open to influence.

(Note: A number of the phrases here are drawn from the work of Judith Glaser on Conversational Intelligence™)

An outcome of this, when implemented by a leader, is that the leader is exerting 'power with' as opposed to 'power over', and new knowledge and ideas are co-created between leader and staff member.

How and if the different positions of the workplace coaching conversational positions are implemented within a setting is highly dependent on the contextual needs of the setting and the people within it. However, we would encourage both leaders and colleagues to actively seek opportunities to both use a coaching approach and to establish more formal coaching interventions wherever possible. Coaching is a great conversational position to adopt to get the very best out of people and enable their growth and development.

At an individual level within SFSE, the opportunity to be engaged in a SF coaching relationship would be highly beneficial. This may be with someone more senior, in years and/or position, where they could also take on a mentoring role, which will be discussed later, or could be in a peer or co-operative colleague coaching model. The evidence of the importance of coaching is now well documented and adopting a SF approach to coaching would further embed SF within the culture of the school. It would also be available to all staff, not just to teachers.

In terms of teams, there is also evidence that adopting a SF Coaching (SFC) approach in a similar setting to special education, where staff were supporting clients with intellectual disability, was very well received.

In the thesis by John Roeden (2012) he identified that the strengths of SFC mentioned by staff included the formulation of a team goal in a positive way, the promotion of self-confidence in the team, the use of competences already present in the team, the focus on solutions-building and the capacity to resolve stagnating care situations. He states that it can be concluded that SFC may be particularly helpful for staff in encouraging positive perspectives, self-confidence, self-efficacy, solutions-building and coping.

Staff reported the following strengths of SFC:

- SFC focuses on successes.

- SFC may promote self-confidence in the team.

- SFC focuses on uniform support of individual clients.

- SFC may provide generalisation from one client to another.

- SFC stimulates reflection of the team.

- SFC offers a step-by-step approach to reach the team goal.

- SFC develops a detailed picture of the team goal.

- SFC uses many approaches to reach a team goal.

- SFC uses competences and workable solutions already present in the team.

- SFC has the capacity to resolve stagnating support situations.

Another SF approach to team coaching that may prove useful is the Solution Circle approach developed by Daniel Meier (2005). The central thought of the Solution Circle is: change happens more sustainably, more dynamically and more effectively when it rests on strengths.

The Solution Circle vision is identified as one of lively, positive, solution and resources-oriented change.

The solution and resource-oriented method opens up the possibility of using tension in the team to develop the team. Turbulence is seen as a positive sign of life.

Meier identifies that working with the Solution Circle in hectic team situations has several advantages:

- By exploring past experiences of success, you attain a more positive picture of yourselves.

- The potential of the team and how it can be used in the future becomes very clear. New images emerge about what this team can yet become. A vision develops which is built on the resources of the team.

- The method creates trust and removes the fear of being embarrassed, criticised or judged.

- The goals and plans for the future developed by the team are based on the resources in the team. The team members gain more confidence in the possibility that the measures agreed upon can actually be carried out since they have experienced elements of them in the past. Thus the likelihood of actually carrying out agreed steps increases.

- Time and energy are concentrated on developing a solution and carrying it out. This saves time.

- We become stronger as we work on our strengths. This is very motivating for the participants, and they enjoy it.

- By concentrating on existing resources, the identity of the team is strengthened.

- It also becomes clear that not everything has to be changed.

As stated previously, these examples should not be seen as 'must-do's' but more as examples of what might be useful in a particular context. The evidence from Roeden's thesis (2012) is particularly relevant given it was from a very similar environment to special education, and Meier suggesting the Solution Circle is useful in 'hectic' team environments resonates with personal experiences in special education environments.

Mentoring

The conversational position we will now explore is the close colleague of coaching, namely mentoring.

There is still much confusion and overlap between coaching and mentoring within the education sector, and more widely from what we have seen. Whilst we do agree with Dr Jim Knight's comment made at the closing plenary of the Australian Coaching in Education Conference in 2015 'At the end of the day, I don't mind what you call it as long as it makes a difference to student outcomes', we do believe that some clarity within organisations is helpful to ensure there is transparency in purpose and roles within conversations.

The definition which, for us, succinctly summarises the role of the mentor is: 'A mentor is a more experienced individual willing to share knowledge with someone less experienced in a relationship of mutual trust' (David Clutterbuck). Therefore, we believe potentially anyone can become a coach but to become a mentor we would need more experience than the colleague we are mentoring. All positions are dependent on the relationship of mutual trust as identified by Clutterbuck.

As identified earlier, whether coaching or mentoring is adopted is dependent on both context and the staff member's knowledge, skills, attitude and experience. Furthermore, it is often appropriate to move from one to the other within a conversation. However, this should be a thoughtful response as opposed to a reactive default response. We have found the 'Know-How Continuum', developed by an excellent SF practitioner and thought leader Dr Mark McKergow, discussed later, to be a useful tool to assist all staff in knowing how to bring their voice to the conversation with colleagues.

As with the coaching conversational position, we believe that within the mentoring conversational position, there is also a continuum where the balance between asking and telling shifts. This has been called the 'Arc of Advice'. Again, this is dependent on context and staff member.

Starting at the right-hand side of the Arc of Advice, the leader would be mainly asking questions and adding their thoughts if they thought it could add value to the staff member. This is most likely to be undertaken with staff with significant knowledge and experience. It is at this right-hand side of the continuum that we believe the blurring between coaching and mentoring is most likely, and that's OK!

Moving along the arc, the balance of input from the mentor is appropriately increasing, so by the time the mentor is at the left-hand side, there will still be some questions but there is a lot more ideas and input from them. This is most likely to be seen with beginning teachers, and for others who are new to their role.

Figure 4.3: The mentoring arc of advice
Source: Burnett (2017)

As just mentioned, a tool that can be really helpful for mentors is the 'Know-How Continuum' from the excellent work of Dr Mark McKergow in his online Solutions Focused Business Professional Course with the University of Wisconsin. Below is an adaptation of this with some suggestions as to the type of questions that could be asked by a mentor in the different spaces.

The 'Know-How Continuum' – adding to the pool of options (adapted from the work of Dr Mark McKergow)
Possible questions

1. Staff member

    i.   What might you do?

    ii. What advice would you give someone else?

    iii. What might I suggest you do?

2. Similar time

    i.   Have you been in a similar situation? What did you do then?

    ii. What worked for you then?

    iii. How might that be of use in this occasion?

3. Someone else

    i.   Is there someone you know who is good at this?

    ii. What do they do?

    iii. What advice might they suggest to you?

Ask permission: Look, I do have some thoughts on this – is it useful for me to share them with you?

4. Third person

    i.   Someone once shared a useful strategy in relation to this with me, they suggested I…

5. Leader – offer at least two options

    i.   What I've found useful is…

    ii. Another thing that might be useful is…

6. Final step: out of all of these options which is the most useful option to start with?

My use of this tool with leaders is to suggest that the more often we can start at the right, the asking space, the better this generally is as leaders are inclined to be ATMs. However, on some occasions, it is highly appropriate for the leader to start somewhere else on the continuum, or recognise the need to move to the left depending on the responses of the staff member – as long as our decision is based on what is of most benefit for the staff member as opposed to what is of most benefit to the leader.

A final note at this stage: I believe it is important, no matter where we start on the continuum or when we decide to move to the left, that, at the 'third person' and 'leader' positions, we ask permission before we share our thoughts or experience. This demonstrates respect for the staff member and is helpful in further building the relationship and trust.

We will now move to the leader/manager position which has been called the Supervisor Conversations See-Saw (Burnett 2017).

Supervisor conversations

As with the other in-school colleague conversational positions, it is suggested that there are a range of Leading Conversations as the leader needs to be constantly adjusting the conversational position depending on the person they are talking to and the need for support or challenge as the major emphasis in the interaction. The Supervisor Conversations See-Saw ranges from Wellbeing to Performance to Compliance, with Performance Conversations, when done well, having both formal and informal elements.

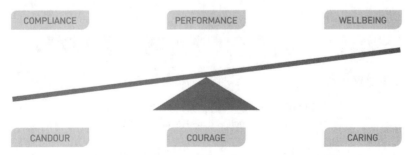

Figure 4.4: Supervisor Conversations See-Saw
Source: Burnett (2017)

At the bottom of the Supervisor Conversations See-Saw, the words CARING – COURAGE – CANDOUR are used. All of these aspects may be needed at any position along the continuum and it is hoped that they represent the basis of the supervisor conversational position: from *caring* to check in with colleagues at a more general level as to how they are travelling; to the *courage* to have the full range of performance conversations; to the *candour* to have the compliance conversations in a way that adds value to the relationship.

We will now explore each of the supervisor conversational positions in a little more detail under the heading of 'Performance Development' (as opposed to performance management) as this sits much more comfortably in a SFSE environment. Unfortunately, there may need to be a performance management aspect with some staff but we have a strong belief if all other elements are done well in the human resources space, these will be infrequent.

Performance Development
Wellbeing

The importance of wellbeing is now being widely recognised within education, for students and also for staff. If staff are not 'in a good space' then how can we expect them to support student wellbeing?

We would suggest that wellbeing in the workplace sits on a scale from −5 (I am in a really bad place with many aspects of work being a real challenge for me) to 0 (I am doing OK at the moment in most aspects of my work) to +5 (I am thriving in my work and often feel in flow) (Csikszentmihalyi, 2004) – see Figure 4.5.

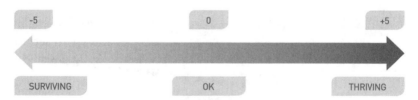

Figure 4.5: The Workplace Wellbeing Scale
Source: Burnett and Montgomery (2018)

There are a range of different approaches and models of wellbeing being used in school environments and we will now explore a model we've been involved in developing called Mojo-Maintenance, which is strongly influenced by both SF and Narrative Therapy.

Mojo-Maintenance

Mojo-Maintenance Training (MMT) is best suited to schools and other workplaces at 0 and above on the Workplace Wellbeing Scale, that is, where staff are already well on their way to creating a positive, supportive staff culture.

MMT is designed to enable participants to train colleagues in the use of 'Peer Reflective Practice' tools to support each other in:

- taking stock of the impacts of the challenging situations they face daily

- sharing ongoing learning about their own resilience and self-regulation.

MMT emerged from the convergence of two streams of work with teams facing challenging human service work.

1. Next Level Greatness (www.nextlevelgreatness.co). Nick Burnett has been working with a range of services, mainly through the Team-Teach[2] behaviour support approach to help these services better support staff to better support clients. As a former principal who has worked in a wide range of school environments, he has many years' experience in training and facilitation.

2. Unique Outcomes (www.uniqueoutcomes.com.au). Amy Stephenson, Paul Montgomery and David Lees have spent the past couple of decades working with staff in domestic and family violence, crisis and emergency, mental health and child protection services to strengthen skills for responding in these challenging fields. They share a commitment to collaboration with service users and other team members as the key ingredient of both sustainable outcomes and enjoyment of work.

During 2016 these streams converged in a pilot project with the team at Nambour Special School. The intention was to create a set of prototype 'tools' for team members to use in supporting each other and sharing reflections on experiences and responses to the everyday challenges

---

2   See www.team-teach.com.au.

of their work. It was hoped this more deliberate and structured way of sharing reflections would lead to team members experiencing a stronger sense of 'felt professional support'.

Following shadowing and consultation with staff in various roles (teacher aides, teachers and leaders) these tools were drafted and road-tested by staff of Nambour Special School with significant positive effects on staff wellbeing.

The 'train the trainer' process created in this project enables participants to use the tools before preparing to introduce them to colleagues.

Why the term 'mojo'?

Many people associate the term 'mojo' with the popular late-1990s 'Austin Powers' movies in which it is associated with particular conceptions of masculinity. A few years ago, we were invited to create a workshop 'to help staff with their mojo'. We were intrigued enough to do a little research on this term and discovered it is much older, traceable back at least as far as the early nineteenth century.

> ...our mojo is that special power or influence that we have, perhaps our unique talent or ability to make things happen, influence others or get things done.
>
> (Barbara Capstick)

These older meanings got us interested in having conversations with colleagues about how they nurture, maintain and restore this sometimes elusive 'mojo' that seems so key to good practice.

We have found colleagues much more interested in talking about 'mojo' than in talking about 'self-care', 'staff wellbeing' or avoiding 'burn-out'. The wry smiles we often see when we introduce the term 'mojo' reflect the principle of 'holding something serious, lightly'.

What is Peer Reflective Practice (PRP)?

PRP is focusing on our own learning, not just on managing stress or challenging behaviour.

In most settings, staff report good organisational responses to both 'critical incidents' in the workplace (e.g. physical or verbal assaults) and the obvious tricky patches in staff members' personal lives (such as loss of a relationship). Nevertheless, most workers recognise that it is the cumulative effect of smaller, day-to-day stresses associated with comparatively low-level challenges that take the bigger toll on their sense of wellbeing and enjoyment of work.

PRP opens space for regular shared focus on these smaller challenges each worker is facing and fosters a culture of 'working out what works' for each worker. Talking with peers about these discoveries, each worker notices the 'distance travelled' as they journey towards their own preferred versions of themselves as workers in these challenging roles.

Why adopt a Peer Reflective Practice (PRP) approach to improving staff wellbeing?

This project has confirmed three key assumptions developed through our work with hundreds of colleagues in a wide variety of settings featuring exposure to challenging situations.

Assumption 1: Sharing responsibility builds resilience and makes people safer

'Staff wellbeing' is often seen as *either* the responsibility of each individual worker, for example, 'that worker needs to get better boundaries to survive this work' or of managers and supervisors, for example, 'the leaders don't adequately support their team'.

We have learned, however, that the active sharing of responsibility, for example, 'each person in the team is keeping an eye out for others and knows how to get timely support from others' contributes to a stronger sense of 'felt professional support' and safer practice. In our experience, these are the workplaces colleagues tend to stay in for longer and in which they say they learn the most.

PRP is a process where supporting staff wellbeing is done *with* people not *to* people.

Assumption 2: It's easier to talk openly when there is less of a power imbalance

In general, workers tend to talk more cautiously to 'the boss' than they do to trusted colleagues with whom they work shoulder to shoulder every day. There are exceptions to this rule but we have found that this is especially true in relation to discussing challenging situations. Fear of performance management/official disciplinary action often contributes to a reticence in discussing both the finer details of workers' responses to challenging situations and the impacts on their levels of stress, coping skills and enjoyment of work.

MMT is designed to leverage this tendency for colleagues to seek the support of and confide more freely in peers and to provide tools to make more conscious and effective use of these peer-to-peer conversations.

Assumption 3: Each of us can develop positive stories of resilience in the face of adversity

We all carry with us the makings of many alternative stories of who we are and how we cope in a range of situations. Some of these potential stories have unhelpful and limiting effects, for example making us see ourselves as inadequate or suffering deficiencies of character. Under the influence of these stories, we can begin to see ourselves and/or other people as 'the problem'.

Other storylines have more helpful potential, for example helping us to remember past successes, lessons learned, cherished values and principles that can help us navigate tricky situations. Under the influence of these stories, we are able to separate ourselves (and others) from 'the problem' and get clearer about our preferred ways of handling challenges.

In the aftermath of tricky situations, the support, feedback and reflections we are offered can make a profound difference in strengthening either the dominant and limiting stories or the more positive and hopeful ones.

MMT is an approach to help individuals create alternative helpful stories of themselves and others.

'Co-constructing' practice wisdom

Instead of each worker developing their own ways of working in isolation, a PRP approach contributes to the sharing of learning so that 'the whole is greater than the sum of the parts'.

Key elements for participation in this collaborative approach to learning include:

- *Being curious* – rather than making assumptions, colleagues become curious 'investigative journalists' helping each other to develop accounts of the ways they are maintaining mojo in the face of significant challenges.

- *Creating a shared understanding* – using the tools with a peer or group of peers helps create a 'meta'-view that can yield new ideas for all involved about responding to tricky situations.

- *Offering empathy instead of sympathy* – instead of only 'sharing the pain' of difficult experiences, the PRP approach encourages all involved to share in developing hopeful possibilities for 'bouncing back' or 'making a come-back' from tough times.

- *Focusing on 'strengths'* – PRP is based on helping staff members identify what they have got to help them maintain or regain their mojo through a range of tools.

Key skills

Effective participation in PRP seems to rely on four key skills that develop quickly with practice.

1. Listening to understand rather than find solutions/offer advice

> *If we speak we only hear what we already know,*
> *if we listen we may learn something new.*

(Dalai Lama)

For PRP to be successful, all involved need to further develop their active listening skills.

Above all, participants aim to connect with each other and understand each other's experiences rather than suggest options and proposals for further action. Through this deeper level of listening we help peers to identify what might be useful for them and where their strengths might be. There is no deeper way to connect to another person than through deep listening where we are displaying compassion and empathy.

2. Asking questions to discover strengths and hopes

> *We live in the world our questions create.*

(David Cooperider)

The questions we ask each other have a significant impact on where we take each other in our thinking and hopes. For this reason, we recommend staff members stay close to the particular types of questions identified in the tools. These questions help identify colleagues' strengths and help step into enabling/helpful 'stories' and reflections rather than stories that can feel 'disabling' or disempowering. It is easy for us to inadvertently stray into questioning that is less helpful and problem focused, and leave colleagues in less helpful spaces.

3. Offering 'resonant' feedback rather than praise or advice

Although praising and complimenting colleagues can be an 'inflater' to Mojo-Maintenance, most colleagues recognise that this is not enough.

In using some of the MMT tools, participants are invited to offer feedback to colleagues about the 'bells that ring' for them as they listen to their colleagues' stories. In general, people find it more useful to hear how their experiences have raised memories of similar or related past experiences rather than be told 'moral tales' of the ways such challenges *should* be handled. These 'resonances' into past experiences often yield new understandings for all parties, not only the colleague whose story stimulated the recollection.

These acknowledgements of resonance are usually experienced as more useful than praise and complimenting in terms of clarifying the ingredients of Mojo-Maintenance or restoration.

4. Journalling

There is increasing evidence (Nguyen, 2017) of the importance and usefulness of journalling, and whilst this is not an expectation in Mojo-Maintenance, it is strongly recommended, and staff members are provided with Mojo-Maintenance journals which have the tools in them as well as space to journal.

It has been found that journalling can assist with:

- mindfulness

- achieving goals

- developing greater emotional intelligence

- improving communication skills

- developing self-confidence

- recovery and healing

- sparking creativity.

(Nguyen, 2017)

As stated, we would suggest that staff wellbeing is both a leadership *and* an individual staff member responsibility, with the major responsibility being to look after ourselves. We also strongly believe that a Peer Reflective Practice model to support wellbeing is the most effective approach as this both shares responsibility with our peers to look after each other and also recognises the potential impact of power as discussed in the first section on 1:1 colleague conversations. It is also crucial to recognise the particular needs of principals, who may have a supportive leadership team but no peers as such within their schools, and a 'spin-off' Mojo-Maintenance for Principals (MMfP) one-day workshop has also been developed with input from members of Queensland Association of Special Education Leaders (QASEL).

We will explore the possible additional support mechanisms needed in SFSE in the 'Additional supports' section of this chapter, but first let's explore a SFSE approach to performance.

Performance

This conversational position on the Supervisor Conversations See-Saw encompasses the full range of 'performance' conversations that leaders may need to undertake. We have a strong belief that in all settings the vast majority of staff are performing to at least a satisfactory level, if not better, and want to improve. Additionally, we do have a strong belief that no one deliberately turns up at work to be worse than they were the day before, even if that is sometimes how it appears. Ensuring that, as leaders, we are undertaking the full myriad of conversations is likely to minimise the number of *compliance* conversations we are likely to need to have.

It has been suggested the performance conversational position has its own continuum, ranging from formal to informal elements. The formal elements are the structured conversations built into the system/ school procedures to reflect on past performance and set goals for future performance, whereas the informal elements are around regular check-ins which will vary from setting to setting. These may include walk-throughs, lesson observations and/or water-cooler conversations. These informal performance conversations may well take the form of coaching and/or mentoring conversational positions.

In settings where performance conversations are done well, there are also planned frequent (at least termly) but brief conversations to explore how staff are travelling and what support they may need to improve.

The name given to performance management has varied widely over the years and also across different systems, for example appraisal and supervision, but we would suggest that in SFSE this is called Performance Development and includes all elements of the Supervisor Conversations See-Saw as opposed to just a focus on performance. Initially we will share some thinking about adopting a SF rating approach suggested by Dr Gunter Lueger (2008).

Solutions Focused Rating (SFR): New ways in performance development

There is evidence that most employees come out of performance appraisals less motivated than when they went in. One of the common factors is that staff are asked to rate their performance over the course of a year on a scale of excellent to poor. The major problem with this approach is that it assumes performance is static whereas in fact this is not the case.

Lueger suggests using 100 points to be distributed across the range of performance indicators with the supervisor then adopting a SF interviewing approach called 'Listening with EARS' developed by Insoo Kim Berg to elicit strengths and competencies on which to build.

Poor	OK	Good	Excellent

Figure 4.6: SFSE Performance Development process

- Staff member reflects on their performance over the last term/semester/year and shares out 100 points across the boxes where they think they have demonstrated that level of performance and makes notes about what they were doing that demonstrated that level of performance, as in Figure 4.6.

- Supervisor asks questions (examples below) and listens with EARS:

  » Elicit – tell me a time when you were at your best.

  » Amplify – tell me more about that. What else?

  » Reinforce – affirm and/or acknowledge the strengths, skills and qualities demonstrated by the staff member.

  » Start Over – tell me another time when you were at your best.

- The supervisor's aim is to get as many examples and as much detail as possible about the staff member operating at their best, and there is also the opportunity to share when the supervisor has noticed times the staff member was operating well.

- When appropriate, the supervisor would then ask 'Suppose you are scoring more to the right-hand side by the end of the next term/semester/year, what could you work on?'

- Then they would move to goal and action setting.

Another Performance Development process that sits well in SFSE is the Five Conversations Framework developed by Dr Tim Baker (2013). The Five Conversations Framework is based on five themed conversations that you have with each of your people, one theme per month, for five months out of six. This means that each topic is covered twice in a year, helping you review their development easily.

A conversation with your team member should last around 15 minutes, and focus on one of the following themes:

- Climate Review: to measure their job satisfaction and morale.

- Strengths and Talents: to identify and develop their innate abilities.

- Opportunities for Growth: to improve their performance and standards.

- Learning and Development: to identify and support future learning opportunities.

- Innovation and Continuous Improvement: to improve their own and your team's effectiveness in line with business needs.

An adaptation we have seen work well around this is a termly focus alongside the annual Solutions Focused Performance Review (SFPR) as opposed to the 'Climate Review'.

Another interesting approach to Performance Development was adopted by Mahlberg and Sjoblom (2004) where it was called supervision. Without referring to the working model the team uses, supervision can proceed from a solution focused perspective. By mapping out well-functioning situations and focusing on the staff's abilities, it is likely that positive patterns will begin to repeat themselves.

To supervise from a solution focused perspective implies that supervision starts with the team's own idea of what they want to use the time for. It is the staff themselves who decides both the focus and the goals. Supervision becomes a collaborative process when you identify what is working and draw attention to the team's resource and competence. The team's own experience and knowledge become the basis for creating new possibilities. The supervisor is not the expert here, but is there to facilitate the team's own thoughts and proposals.

Characteristic of the solution focused approach is that the supervisor will also ask questions reflecting the perspectives of third parties:

- 'How will the pupils want things to be?'

- 'What are the parents' views about this?'

As stated at the outset of this section on Performance Development, we have a strong belief that the vast majority of staff are performing at least at a satisfactory level, or better, and want to improve. However, there may be some who are not and this leads into the compliance end of the Supervisor Conversations See-Saw.

Compliance

This end of the see-saw is reserved for those conversations which are about holding staff accountable to system/school expectations and when staff are not meeting these. This could be for a range of reasons and these are often framed as 'difficult' conversations. If done with caring, courage and candour these can actually lead to improved relationships.

In an ideal world, leaders would not need to have these conversations. Whilst we are not in an ideal world, if all other conversations are done well we do believe there will need to be very few of these conversations.

Additional supports

Intervision

Intervision is a 'peer coaching' activity with a small group of professionals or managers who have a professional context or challenge in common. It is a similar concept to that of MMT Peer Reflective Practice discussed earlier, but the focus here is on professional practice as opposed to wellbeing.

The term 'Intervision' emphasises the multilateral exchange between colleagues as opposed to supervision.

It is an opportunity to use each other's vision, experience and ideas in order to find new ways of addressing issues in your work context. In summary, Intervision is:

- intercolleagial consulting

- in a work context

- with colleagues, equals (it is not the formal hierarchy that is important, but the felt freedom to speak up and show weakness)

- with a simple format and structure (and within a short time frame)

- as an important trigger for experiential learning.

CASE STUDY: **SOLUTION FOCUSED INTERVISION**

Paut Kromkamp, Rob Paludanus and Marieke Wulffraat

'Intervision' is the word we use for a structured way in which participants in a group or team coach each other, as it were, on work-related issues. Intervision can be used in case consultations, by a team that wishes to adopt new practices, in management teams that would like to coach each other, as a way to practise and further your Solution Focused skills and to be inspired by like-minded others. Groups consist ideally of five to eight or ten people, but larger groups are also possible with some modifications. Members can all have the same role or position in one company or they can come from varying backgrounds and/or jobs, depending on the goals and wishes of the group. In appreciative (focused on what is going well) or Solution Focused organisations, the manager or team leader is often a member of the team Intervision group.

Participants describe the Intervision sessions as fun and to the point. They furthermore stated that their understanding was deepened, their confidence in their Solution Focused skills improved and that the skill and team building contributed to the change they wished to see in their organisations.

At Vraagkracht (an SF consultancy) we use a variety of Solution Focused Intervision models. In the following section we've described one that is always very popular and that shows the possibilities of Intervision. Other models we frequently use are called Positive Gossip, Three Columns (as used in Signs of Safety and Signs of Wellbeing), Resource Detective (thanks to Peter Szabo), A Trip To The Museum (thanks to Chris Iveson), PSPT (Problem, Suggestions, Plan, Tips) and others.

The six steps model

One group member at a time gets to put their question or dilemma to the group. This question or dilemma is then discussed by the group, in a structured manner, with the aim of helping their colleague acquire new and useful ideas.

Facilitator: mandated by the group to guide the process.

Colleague: the person putting his or her question to the table.

Italics: for the facilitator.

Normal: for the participants.

Within quotation marks ('): ask literally.

Numbered: ask the questions in that order.

Bullets: choose from or make your own variation.

1. The question or dilemma

- What is the reason behind your question?

- Tell us about your dilemma

- What is your main reason for asking this question?

2. Brief elaboration

'Could you describe to us, in five to ten sentences max, the context of your question? Talk about things that might be useful for us to know, so that we can give you the suggestions that will be most useful to you.'

'At the end, please ask your question again. See if you can start your question with: 'How can I...' or: 'Help me to...'

3. Clarifying questions

'All of us get the chance to ask (one/your very best) question that you think might be really useful for our colleague. The idea is not to go for facts, but to focus on what would be most helpful for your colleague.'

- What have you done so far that worked?

- On a scale of 1 to 10 (1 being: 'I am totally at the beginning' and 10 being: 'yes, I can close the case/the project is finished successfully/...'), where are you now?

- Suppose a colleague were to ask you this question, what advice would give him or her?

- What solutions for your dilemma have you thought of yourself?

- What have you tried so far that has not worked?

- You clearly have thought about this a lot. What ideas have you come up with already?

- What did you do in earlier situations like this that worked?

- Suppose we don't come up with the right ideas, who else could you ask?

Facilitator:

- *How have our questions so far been useful?*

- *What questions would you have liked us to ask that we didn't?*

- *Would you like to rephrase your question at this time? What would it be now?*

4. Appreciation round

'Briefly tell your colleague the one thing that impressed you the most about him or her, based on what you just heard, such as:

- I admire…

- I am impressed by…

- I envy how you…

It's OK to repeat a compliment.

The colleague who asked the question to the group just listens and does not respond!'

5. Tips and ideas
(To the colleague who asked the question to the group) Just listen and write down what makes you curious and what you might want to remember.

(To the rest of the group) Give your colleague your tip or idea in a concrete and clear way, in one sentence, starting for example with:

- I would…

- Remember…

- You could read…

- Go and talk to…

'Let the group go several rounds. Ask the colleague with the question after a while if he or she has heard things that could be useful. Or you could continue till everyone has run out of suggestions.'

6. Reflection by the person with the question
'On a scale of 1 to 10, where 1 is: 'this was a total waste of time', and 10 is: 'this was the best decision I could have made today, to ask you guys this question', where on the scale would you say you are right now?'

And perhaps you would like to ask something like: what could we have said that would have made it just a tiny bit higher?

Note: the rest of the group does not ask any more questions or add tips or suggestions at this point. Thank you's all around and on to the next question. Have fun!

Supporting staff facing regular crises

Whilst many staff in SFSE are highly skilled in the de-escalation of dangerous behaviours, there are occasions when they are likely to face regular violent and aggressive incidents.

We believe that Mojo-Maintenance is a highly useful approach for all staff that face regular lower-level (in terms of risk) behaviours but the focus of this section is on the significant incidents, often called 'critical incidents'.

Whilst violent attacks can be particularly difficult to deal with, little is known about the effects on those who have to deal with them. Indeed we were only able to find one research study into this area by Howard and Hegarty (2003) and so we will draw heavily on the findings from this research as well as our experience in working in such a setting, and our ongoing work in supporting and training staff who work in such settings.

The paper by Howard and Hegarty (2003) had three aims:

1. To describe the experiences and emotional reactions of staff to violent incidents.

2. To examine the effects of violence on the teaching and care relationship that staff members have with children.

3. To establish what factors influence emotional reactions to violence.

Our focus is particularly on the second aim as this is crucial to being able to work in a restorative way.

From Howard and Hegarty's review of the limited literature, there were some particularly relevant findings in relation to Restorative Practice (RP). Violence towards staff is costly to services in terms of staff absence, stress and resignations (Rose, 1995). The experience of stress may account for the high staff turnover seen in learning disability services, although Rose (1995) points out that high staff turnover may actually be a positive way of losing less functional members. Staff experiencing stress are far less likely to interact with clients (Rose, Jones and Fletcher, 1993). This therefore has implications for the building of relationships between staff and the client.

Additionally, Smith and Hart (1994) noted that emotional reactions were heightened where attacks were perceived as personal. The six participants in the research were working in a residential special school for children with Intellectual Disability (ID) and seriously challenging behaviour in the UK. From the interviews there were seven emergent themes:

1. The physical force of the violence

2. Staff reactions to violence

3. Acceptance of violence

4. The importance of support from the staff team

5. Coping strategies used by staff

6. The effect of violence on relationships between staff and students

7. Mediators of staff reaction to violence:

   i.   Personal factors

   ii. Perception of violence

   iii. Characteristics of the violent situation

   iv. School's attitude to violence

We are going to particularly focus on number six as this is obviously a crucial element to the restorative process.

The effect of violence on relationships between staff and students

From the study commentary it is reported that this produced contradictory opinions. Many of the staff felt that the clients' violence towards them had no effect on the relationship because they didn't allow it to. Some staff, however, felt that there was an effect on the relationship and that it could cause anxiety around clients, or make staff feel that they didn't want to work with the client, although this tended to be a reaction to more extreme cases of violence. One member of staff felt that staff reactions to violence provided an opportunity to improve the relationship with the client, through creating trust and boundaries. However, of those staff who felt violence affected the relationship, most felt that this was a negative effect. Staff also suggested that the clients were very perceptive and therefore their knowledge of the staff's feelings could also affect the relationship.

The experience of violence was affected by factors prior to the event, the event itself, and what happened afterwards – see Figure 4.7.

PRE-INCIDENT	INCIDENT	POST-INCIDENT
Experience	Characteristics of violence	Supported by other staff
Attitudes	Who the client is	Coping style
Training	Violence expected	Emotional resilience
School attitude to violence	Staff support available	Opportunity to talk and express emotions
Professional attitude	Perceived ability to cope	
Personal factors	Level of injury	

Figure 4.7: The effect of violence on relationships between staff and students
Source: Adapted from Howard and Hegarty (2003)

Whilst many of the factors identified in the figure are personal factors, there are a number that are setting and leadership factors, such as training, attitude of the school to violence, staff support available at the time of the incident and post incident, and having debriefing processes in place to support staff.

Even though, to some extent, not all individuals are going to be suited to working in such environments, it cannot and should not be left to just whether the staff member has the required personal characteristics to cope. Leadership in such settings is crucial in ensuring that violence does not just become an accepted part of the job, and either 'you can cope or find a different job'.

Violence causes emotional reactions that are stressful. Staff training and support can help minimise the effect on staff. We believe there's a crucial role for training in, and the use of, RP in meeting this need. This is particularly powerful when delivered alongside whole-school holistic training that helps staff to take a positive approach to dealing with violent incidents, as well as giving them the necessary skills to reduce the chance of harm to themselves or the individuals displaying the violence. Settings should foster mutual support in staff teams and allow opportunities for staff to have time out during working hours, as well as being offered additional support as needed.

Debriefing

One element of staffing that may be different in special education than most general education settings is that of staff being faced with numerous incidents of severe challenging behaviour. Where this occurs there needs to be high levels of support for both the children and the staff.

In relation to staff, adopting a SF approach to debriefing is likely to help staff feel more supported and identify ways forward rather than be stuck in the problem. This is not easy and in many situations it may be important for the staff member to share the difficulties and problems they face before moving on to possible solutions that may work in the future. If this level of support is needed for the staff member and/or others adopting a restorative approach it would seem to be a good fit in terms of acknowledging the harm, but then moving on to examining possible ways forward. Within the field of special education, adopting a restorative approach is often more challenging and further guidance on adopting this approach is available in the book *Restorative Practice and Special Needs* (Burnett and Thorsborne, 2015). In incidents where acknowledging the harm is not as useful then using SF approaches to interviewing as mentioned earlier could be a useful approach.

Conclusion

This chapter contains a number of examples/approaches that have been used/developed within a SF context. We would want to reiterate that adopting a SF approach means that these should not be seen as 'answers' but more as examples of 'what's working' or 'what might work' in some settings.

Changing cultures is one of the most complex challenges that face leaders in all settings but, by adopting a SF approach, we would suggest that things can move forward one conversation at a time.

References

Baker, T. (2013) *The End of the Performance Review. Winners at Work.* London: Palgrave Macmillan.

Burnett, N. (2017) 'The spectrum of leadership conversations – Part One: in-school colleague conversational positions – coaching.' Available at www.linkedin.com/pulse/spectrum-leadership-conversations-part-one-in-school-nick-burnett (accessed 2/10/2018).

Burnett, N. and Montgomery, P. (2018) 'What is mojo and why maintain it?' Available at www.linkedin.com/pulse/what-mojo-why-maintain-nick-burnett (accessed 2/10/2018).

Burnett, N. and Thorsborne, M. (2015) *Restorative Practice and Special Needs.* London: Jessica Kinglsey Publishers.

Csikszentmihalyi, M. (2004) *Good Business: Leadership, Flow and the Making of Meaning.* Harmondsworth: Penguin Books.

Howard, R. and Hegarty, J.R. (2003) 'Violent incidents and staff stress.' *The British Journal of Developmental Disabilities,* 49(1), 3–21.

Lueger, G. (2008) *Solution Focused Rating (SFR): New Ways in Performance Appraisal.* Available at https://epdf.tips/solution-focused-management.html (accessed 22/10/2018).

Mahlberg, K. and Sjoblom, M. (2004) *Solution Focused Education.* Stockholm: Mareld.

Meier, D. (2005) *Team Coaching with the Solution Circle.* Cheltenham: Solutions Books.

Nguyen, T. (2017) '10 surprising benefits you'll get from keeping a journal.' Available at www.huffingtonpost.com/thai-nguyen/benefits-of-journaling-_b_6648884.html (accessed 2/10/2018).

Norman, H, Pidsley, T. and Hjerth, M. (2005) 'Solution focused reflecting teams in action.' In M. McKergow and J. Clarke (eds) *Positive Approaches to Change: Applications of Solutions Focus and Appreciative Inquiry at Work.* Cheltenham: Solutions Books.

Roeden, J. (2012) *Solution Focused Support of People with Intellectual Disabilities.* Available at www.kennispleingehandicaptensector.nl/images/beteroud/nieuws/SFBT%20-%20proefschrift%20Roeden.pdf (accessed 2/10/2018).

Röhrig, P. and Clarke, J. (eds) (2008) *57 SF Activities for Facilitators and Consultants: Putting Solutions Focus into Action.* Cheltenham: Solutions Books.

Rose, J. (1995) 'Stress and residential staff: towards an integration of existing research.' *Mental Handicap Research,* 8, 220–235.

Rose, J., Jones, F. and Fletcher, B. (1993) 'Investigating the relationship between stress and worker behaviour.' *Journal of Intellectual Disability Research,* 42, 163–172.

Smith, M.E., and Hart, G.H. (1994) 'Nurses' responses to patient anger: from disconnecting to connecting.' *Journal of Advanced Nursing,* 20, 643–651.

van Nieuwerburgh, C. (2016) 'Coaching in education.' In T. Bachkirova, G. Spence and D. Drake *The SAGE Handbook of Coaching.* London: Sage.

Chapter 5

SOLUTIONS FOCUSED SPECIAL EDUCATION TEACHING AND LEARNING PROCESSES

Nick Burnett and Jenny Cole

Introduction

The focus of this chapter is on the teaching and learning processes within special education. The planning, delivery and reviewing of teaching and learning will be explored, drawing on a number of examples from Kerstin Mahlberg and Maud Sjoblom's book on Solution Focused Education (2004) and more recent work by Thomas Armstrong on neurodiversity (2012). We will also share a detailed outline of suggested person-centred planning approaches.

Finally, we will also share some thoughts on further developing teaching practices through adopting Solutions Focused (SF) approaches to the training of mentors and a suggested lesson observations format.

The premise of this chapter is that we continually construct and reconstruct our knowledge, actions and arrangements in our everyday conversations. This is a form of action learning in which we use insightful questions to consider our activities and experiences in the light of our existing knowledge. If our conversations and processes are SF, we believe it opens up avenues as to what is possible and recognises strengths as opposed to the current focus of deficit in a number of current special education teaching and learning processes.

For Insoo Kim Berg, language did not reflect reality, it actively created it.

SF approach to learning and support planning

From our experiences as special education teachers and principals there may be challenges as to how we access the views of a number of students that we have been involved with over the years. However, we are of the strong view that this should not stop us trying to find ways to access and use their knowledge of themselves, and they often find ways of giving us feedback as to what is and what isn't working by their behaviour!

Finding better ways of examining how we can use the observable behaviours of those we are supporting to identify strengths and abilities, as opposed to difficulties and problems, is no doubt a challenge with some of the more complex individuals within special education settings, but is a fundamental value of adopting a SF approach to special education.

We would also want to acknowledge the importance of professional input which may come from a range of associated people depending on the individual. However, in adopting a SFSE approach we believe that their recommendations should be reframed as suggestions. As stated earlier, Insoo Kim Berg identified the importance of the words used is significant and so seeing professional input as 'suggestions' as opposed to 'must follow' is an important step. The key is involving all the 'experts', including family and friends, as much as possible and seeing all viewpoints as equally valid. The role of parents, families and friends is a crucial element in developing appropriate teaching and learning strategies, and these should be seen as an important resource.

As the process of planning, teaching, reviewing and redesigning should be implemented in an ongoing cyclical process with each informing the next stage, these should not be examined separately.

In the following section we will explore the process developed by Mahlberg and Sjoblom in their special school and then examine elements of planning, teaching and reviewing from other sources of interest, with some additional suggestions in italics added by ourselves.

The Mellansjo School Process

Mahlberg and Sjoblom's (2004) book on Solution Focused Education explores a number of processes that worked in their setting, Mellansjo School.

This should be viewed as an example of what worked in their setting with their students and should not be seen as the way to implement this approach. One of the basic principles of working in a SF way is that *every case is different*.

Fundamental to the model described by Mahlberg and Sjoblom is that teacher, pupil and parent 'build' a solution together rather than solve a problem. We would see this as a crucial element and as a starting point with all students, although the student level of involvement may vary and we would also include significant others such as the support staff who work closely with the student.

Steps

1. The teacher helps the pupil *(and family)* to 'envision' and describe the situation as it will be when the problem is solved and the trouble is gone.

2. The teacher is to find out what the pupil *(and family)* is already doing which shows that they have taken a step in that direction.

3. Find out what else is required, what the pupil can do to get another small step closer to their goal – then parents and school staff.

4. Give the pupil *(and family)* plenty of positive feedback for the things they are already doing that are taking them in the right direction.

In SF terms, the steps would be described as identifying the following:

1. A 'preferred future' – where preferred future is how the pupil and family want things to be.

2. What's working – when are the times the pupil is already achieving elements of the preferred future, and what might we learn from these instances.

3. Even better when... – identify what the next steps might be for the pupil, family and school staff to move closer to the preferred future.

4. Affirming – acknowledging and affirming the pupil and the family for what they've already achieved, including identifying strengths and resources that will help them achieve the preferred future. It can also be highly beneficial for school leaders to recognise these for the class staff working closely with the pupil.

Noticing positive change

The question 'What is better now?' is one of the most common introductory questions in solution focused assessment and review meetings.

The SF focus is on 'what's working' rather than 'what isn't', and a useful follow-up question is 'How did you manage to do that?' If this is not something we are able to elicit easily from the student, we would suggest the exact same questions are explored with staff and parents.

The next stage would be revisiting the steps again. In relation to the 'preferred future' step, once our minds have constructed a positive image of the future, the possibility of living it becomes so much greater. This is another important element in adopting a SF approach to teaching and learning processes in special education settings. This may well be framed as goals or aspirations to move towards.

Progress assessment meetings

The following examples of scaling headings aim to build a picture of how satisfied the pupil (*with family input as is helpful*) is with their school situation, what already works well, and eventually what needs to be improved.

The pupil (*with family input as is helpful*) is asked to grade where they are on the scale in relation to the desired state which is defined as a '10' while '0' defines the opposite situation:

- Feeling good in school

   » 10 = I am very happy.

- The breaks

   » 10 = The breaks are fun.

- Relationships with friends.

   » 10 = I am a good friend.

- Individual planning

   » 10 = I always complete my tasks.

- My schoolwork

   » 10 = I work as hard as I can.

- The school building

  » 10 = Very good rooms and facilities.

- The atmosphere

  » 10 = Great atmosphere in class.

Action plans

At FKC Mellansjo, they chose to adopt action plans as opposed to the traditional type of pupil reports which often have more to say about what the pupil cannot do, than what they can do. Instead of using a deficit model as their template, they wanted action plans to record achievement not failure, strengths not weaknesses, and proactive measures not reactive ones.

However, to be able to devise an action plan effectively, they felt they needed an accurate mapping of what is happening now – an understanding of the pupil's present state.

Educational mapping

They felt that the mapping should contain statements about:

- the pupil's strengths and earlier successes
- when things work best for the pupil
- teaching methods used
- the approach adopted (adult–pupil–adult)
- descriptions of the teaching and learning environment
- the social context
- the quality of co-operation between the home and the school.

Other important elements to the process at Mellansjo School
Reframing

To encourage our pupils and parents to look at a problem from another point of view, we use reframing. With positive reframing the possibility of finding new solutions increases.

Asking 'when…' in place of 'if…'

The word when implies that the pupil has the ability to achieve, and by using when, the teacher makes it clear that s/he believes in the pupil's ability to do it.

Working with parents

At Mellansjo School the parents are very much viewed as a resource. The parents are in school with their children for the first ten days, and after that they spend one day, half a day or a week in school every term, for as long as their child is enrolled.

The responsibility for initiating and continuing this dialogue lies with the school. All teachers are supported and helped to know how to manage their contacts with parents and how to deal with possible conflict.

At Mellansjo School there is a strong belief that no parent should ever have to leave a meeting feeling offended or upset. They believe in having a shared responsibility for making parents feel comfortable whether in formal meetings or informal conversation.

As stated at the start of this section, and we're sure that Mahlberg and Sjoblom would agree, given their significant work in the field of Solution Focused Education, the process should not be seen as a recipe, more an example of how the key ingredients were put together to best meet the needs of the students they were supporting.

We will now go on to explore some other interesting thoughts that have relevance to SFSE teaching and learning processes.

Neurodiversity

The first we are going to explore is that of neurodiversity as developed by Thomas Armstrong (2012). The idea of neurodiversity is, in the words of Thomas Armstrong, a revolutionary new concept in special education that employs a positive 'diversity' perspective similar to biodiversity and cultural diversity to replace the current 'disability' discourse that prevails in today's educational circles.

Armstrong describes neurodiversity as essentially an ecological perspective, and therefore also develops a related concept of positive niche construction – that is, the establishment of a favourable environment within which a student with special needs can flourish in school.

Armstrong identifies seven components for positive niche construction, including:

1. A comprehensive assessment of a student's strengths.

2. The use of assistive technologies and 'universal design' for learning methodologies.

3. The provision of enhanced human resources.

4. The implementation of strength-based learning strategies.

5. The envisioning of positive role models.

6. The activation of affirmative career aspirations.

7. The engineering of appropriate environmental modifications to support the development of neurodiverse students.

To assist in positive niche construction, Armstrong has developed a very detailed Neurodiversity Strengths Checklist which has 14 areas of focus:

- personal
- communication
- emotional
- cognitive
- creative
- literacy
- logical
- visual-spatial
- dexterity
- musical
- nature
- high-tech
- spiritual
- cultural.

We do believe that the concept of neurodiversity has much to offer the developing discussion regarding SFSE. As with the examples from Mellansjo School, we do not see it as having all the answers but it could have some more of the ingredients to use with certain students at certain times and is certainly helpful in reframing the discussion in special education away from deficit.

Armstrong, in his book, also refers to an interesting Individual Education Plan (IEP) process, which comes from an Appreciative Inquiry (AI) frame of reference (Kozik, 2008). Those of you who are more familiar with SF will be aware that there are many complementary beliefs between SF and AI.

The AI-IEP Protocol basically has three elements:

1. Successes – what things have been going well for the student.

2. Goals – what are the next goals that are most appropriate for the student.

3. Support – what supports does the student need to give them the best chance of success in achieving these goals in terms of teaching approaches, etc.

It can be seen that this has a number of similarities to the earlier action planning process from Mellansjo School. We will now go on to share a range of person-centred SF practices for planning for students with special needs.

Person-centred practices in school: a SF approach to planning for students with special needs

Many planning paradigms for children and young people with special needs are deficit based with the individual seen as a range of conditions to be fixed or problems to be solved. When planning meetings are arranged, they are often done so to comply with legislation with the focus of the agenda to fix weaknesses in the students' academic, therapeutic or behavioural domains. On the other hand, person-centred planning seeks to:

1. Craft a vision for a person's life as part of their local community and/or the broader mainstream of life.

2. Describe the actions needed to move it in that direction (National Disability Authority, 2012).

It accomplishes this through:

- discovering and responding effectively to the various aspirations, capacities and concerns of individuals with disabilities

- understanding and addressing the core issues for individuals – exploring where the person is now, how they would like their life to change and what bringing about that change might entail

- identifying and exploring choices available to the individual

- mobilising and involving individuals' entire social networks as well as resources from the system of statutory services in responding to what is expressed, and helping to bring about whatever changes are desired

- making arrangements to follow up on plans on a regular basis in order to go through them, review progress on putting them into action and update them

- discovering a way to record, on an ongoing basis:

  » what has been learned about what is important *to* an individual and what is important for them

  » what *balance* has been worked out between what is important to the person and what is important for *them*

- where there is a conflict between the two:

  » what others are expected to know about what is important to and for the person and/or what others are expected to do to help the person get what is important to and for them

  » what needs to stay the same and what needs to change – and who will do what (by when) in acting on these

  » what is, in fact, staying the same and what is changing following the development of a person-centred plan – and whether this is making a real difference to the person's life in either case.

Individual Education Plan process – using a SF approach

The approach which will now be described can be time and labour intensive so is recommended to be held on entry to the school and then at transition points, approximately every three years. Other meetings held each semester may only include a core group from the support team.

Before the meeting

- Determine who should be involved. This should involve the student, his parents, caregivers, current and new teachers, support agencies including therapy, medical, community or work access, grandparents or significant family members.

- Schedule a time. Some meetings, particularly those focused on school to life transition, can take several hours.

- Determine the facilitator. This person is responsible for implementing the SF process, including charting responses on flipcharts.

- Encourage and brief parents/participants prior to the meeting. Send out agendas and information about the SF process you will be using prior to the meeting. This could include asking participants to consider the student's strengths and aspirations.

At the meeting

- Welcome and introduce all participants.

- Introduce the purpose of the meeting. Each meeting will have an overall purpose such as 'Transition to High School planning' meeting or a review meeting. The facilitator should also establish some understandings of solution focused person-centred planning terminology and philosophy such as:

  » an aspirational approach – what does the student want for himself and what do we, as his support network, want – as opposed to what we don't want

  » a focus on what is working, including the use of SF rating scales as appropriate

  » the role of the facilitator.

- The person-centred planning process, especially Future Perfect, may seem confrontational for parents. Acknowledge to the group that strong emotions are likely and that this group is a safe place where our only aim is to support the young person to lead their best possible life.

- Follow a format or agenda. A suggested format will follow.

- At the end of the meeting:

  » review what has been discussed and charted

  » repeat the agreements and actions, allocating responsibilities as required

  » Inform participants of when a copy of the meeting notes and/or IEP will be available for final consideration.

Generic meeting format

1. What are the long-term aims for the student? 'Miracle Question' (see below).

2. What are the child's strengths, attributes, interests and competencies?

3. What should be the focus for the next 12–18 months?

4. What can be achieved this semester?

5. What role does everyone agree to play?

6. How shall we review and when?

SF strategies to be used in the meeting
(Words in italic are suggested 'scripts'.)

1. What are the long-term aims for the student?
The Miracle Question[1] – adapted. When planning for students with special needs the facilitator should not make any reference to the 'Miracle

---

1   See https://en.wikipedia.org/wiki/Solution-focused_brief_therapy#The_miracle_question.

Question' as it often leads participants to focus on a 'cure' for the student's disability rather than establish a preferred future.

Procedure

The facilitator gives everyone eight post-it notes and encourages participants to arrange them in a grid in front of them. The facilitator reads out the following question slowly, encouraging group members to silently jot down answers to the questions asked on the post-it notes – one answer per note. Participants are not obliged to write and are welcome to fill more than eight notes. They are to answer from their own point of view, with no right or wrong answers. There will be time for discussion later.

Note: unless the student is very medically fragile, or has a degenerative condition, we highly encourage the group to focus on what we want for the child as an *adult* so that we project and 'dream' post-school. The questions can be modified to fit the child's context.

Facilitator:

Let's imagine that we close our eyes and go to sleep.

We have the best sleep ever and wake up refreshed. Somehow overnight many years have gone past and all of a sudden Daniel is 25. You are not sure how you know it is X years into the future – all you know is that Dan is happy and healthy, and he is leading the best possible life. It's like a movie and you are watching his life and yours – like a drone flying above and through the story.

Just keep thinking about Daniel as a young adult – it's first thing in the morning on a typical day.

Where is Daniel, what is he doing? He's getting ready for the day – jot down what you see.

Who is with Daniel? Maybe no one.

Is he eating breakfast? Maybe he's just been to the gym or for a ride. Where did he go, who did he go with?

Don't forget that Dan is leading his best possible life – so if you have thoughts like 'He can't go anywhere on his own' I want you to turn that into 'He has a great young carer who goes to the gym with him.'

Dan starts to get ready for the day. Where might he be going on this awesome day, and how do you think he will be getting there? Write down what you see, what you think, what you hear.

Now Dan is here for the day. Where is he, what's he doing, who's he with? Where did he sit or stand during the day? Did he stay in one place or was he in a number of locations?

If he is with others, what are they talking about, and what are they feeling?

It may feel silly but what did he have for lunch, and where did lunch come from?

The sun starts to go down – where is Dan now? Who is he with? What is he doing?

What else is he doing?

What else?

Tell me about his friends, his family, his relationships.

Facilitator: *Now I am going to give you a couple of quiet minutes to finish off jotting any thoughts or ideas. Make as many post-it notes about Dan's best possible life as you can think of.*

Get the team into groups of three or four:

Have a quick chat about what each of you saw for Daniel, talk about where he was living, how he was occupying his time etc.

Join all the notes together and group the notes into themes. Discuss.

Each group quickly reports back about how they saw Daniel at 25 and any themes they came up with.

The facilitator now leads the discussion, as most groups will report back versions of the same themes dependent on the ability of each student.

Using the words the groups come up with, chart the major themes and reread to the group.

So we are agreed, when Daniel is 25 our wish for him is that he...

When Daniel is 25 he will:

- *live away from the family home*

- *be as independent as possible with daily living tasks*

- *have friends/relationships*

- *be safe/happy/well looked after*

- *be able to manage his own money or have enough money/funding*

- *drive/use transport/get around as independently as possible.*

The facilitator congratulates the group on the list and then discusses the fact that we are all responsible for preparing the student for adulthood and for doing these things on the chart, whether we are teachers, parents or therapists; these are our long-term aims.

It is also useful to help the group see that this is only X number of years into the future and that there are only Y number of years left at school so we need to stay focused. The next step is being clear on where we are now.

SF RATING SCALE[2]

In some instances it may be useful to use a SF rating scale at this point.

If what we have just described for Daniel is perfect, just awesome – it's a 10/10, his very best life:

- *Where are we now on a scale of 1–10?*

- *What's working to make it an X out of 10?*

Explore what is working until a list is created.

2. What are the child's strengths, attributes, interests and competencies?

The facilitator charts what Daniel can already do.

On flipcharts around the room, have headings such as:

- academic skills

- independent living skills/competencies

- social skills

- home/family

- hobbies, obsessions, rewards, likes and dislikes.

Either individually, in pairs or as a whole group, relentlessly pursue what is working by asking questions:

- What can Daniel do? What else can he do?

- What does he like? What else does he like?

- Who or what will he work for? Who else?

---

2   See https://en.wikipedia.org/wiki/Solution-focused_brief_therapy#Scaling_questions.

3. What should be the focus for the next 12–18 months?

Using the information gathered thus far, the facilitator attempts to capture the medium-term focus using SF strategies such as:

- If we could focus on two to three things in the next 12 months that would make the most difference to the child, what would they be?

- If we are currently at a 5/10 on our rating scale, what would take us to a 6?

- What do we (as a support team) need to stop doing to ensure Daniel meets his goals?

4. What can be achieved this semester?

This is similar to Question 3 except the facilitator aims to get specific about measurable and achievable behavioural outcomes. Questions could include versions of the following:

- What could we teach to mastery this semester?

- If we could tick one thing off as achieved in the next ten or 20 weeks what would that be?

- What would we see if this term/semester has been successful?

- What would the data say if this term/semester has been successful?

- If this term/semester has been successful, how many of Daniel's IEP goals have been achieved?

5. What role does everyone agree to play?

The meeting may have decided that independence is a major priority for Daniel, particularly toileting and dressing. The group may spend some time coming to agreements about the roles of the parents, school, teachers, therapists and outside agencies in this goal. These agreements will be recorded; however, the school's IEP document will only contain those targets that are teachable and measurable at school. This part of the process also establishes champions – individuals on the team whose role it is to make sure that the focus is maintained in certain areas.

Questions may include:

- What can we (as a support team) focus on?

- What do we (as individuals or as a team) need to do more of?

- What do we (as individuals or as a team) need to stop doing?

- How do we have to be to ensure Daniel meets his goals?

- Who would like to champion elements of Daniel's medium-term plan?

CASE STUDY: BEN – AN EXAMPLE OF LOOKING FOR A CHILD'S STRENGTHS

Ben is a six-year-old boy who lives on a farm, 20 kilometres from a small rural community in Western Australia. He attends his local government primary school with his two school-aged brothers. His father is a farmer, his mother is a homemaker and they have two other children who are not yet of school age.

Ben is quiet and shy and struggles to keep up at school; he seems inattentive and his teacher reports he is often 'away with the fairies'. After 18 months of full-time schooling he is yet to master all letter sounds and still relies heavily on pictures and context cues to understand his home readers. It is difficult to gauge his comprehension as he is very reluctant to answer questions.

At the case conference meeting the parents did not appear to have high aspirations for Ben saying: 'He'll just work for me on the farm and his mum will look after him.' The facilitator tried very hard to make a list of things that Ben could do, but his young teacher was not very positive and questions such as 'Does he make his own lunch or get himself dressed?' were just met with answers like 'Nah, I am in too much of a rush in the morning – I just do it for him.'

The facilitator asked out of curiosity 'Does he catch the bus to school in the morning?' and Dad responded, 'Yeah, he and his brothers drive to the neighbour's gate and catch the bus from there.'

'He drives?'

'Yeah, he takes the old farm ute, sticks it in second and bunny hops all the way to the front gate.'

Suddenly, a six-year-old child who could 'do nothing' had the start of a positive plan – he could drive a car and he apparently loved to help his father tinker in the shed.

Now the planning team were able to build a list of strengths, interests and talents around mechanics, and in turn the school-based staff could differentiate curricula and design teaching materials to be more motivating.

The final source of resources to assist in adopting a SFSE approach to teaching and learning processes is drawn from the work of Helen Sanderson Associates (HSA).[3] Helen Sanderson Associates have been one of the key organisations in the developing work on Personalising Education,[4] which has been developed for all schools to help them implement person-centred practices.

These resources include processes and paperwork around a number of themes which have been designed to be accessible by many students in special education settings; they would not need much adapting for them to be accessible to virtually all students as they are, and can be, highly visual.

The documents, penned by teachers, practitioners and educational psychologists, whilst not fully fitting the SF paradigm, describe 14 person-centred thinking tools and practices that can bring enormous benefits to schools and colleges:

- appreciation
- one-page profiles
- Communication Chart 1 – how the pupil communicates with us
- Communication Chart 2 – how we communicate with the pupil
- learning log
- good day/bad day
- 4 plus 1 questions
- working and not working from different perspectives
- relationship circle
- decision-making
- community contributions
- roles and responsibilities (the Doughnut)

---

3   See www.helensandersonassociates.co.uk.
4   See www.personalisingeducation.org.

- matching

- person-centred reviews.

The person-centred review is based on the Year 9 transition reviews which are required in the UK, but you can see from the following headings that there are a number of areas that would fit the SFSE context and that others would only need minimal re-working:

- who's here?

- progress on actions

- what we appreciate about…

- important to…now

- important to…in the future

- how best to support

- questions to answer

- working/not working

  » person

  » family

  » staff

  » other

- outcomes and actions in relation to:

  » working

  » not working

  » important in the future

  » questions to answer.

A SF approach to improving teaching and learning

The following section is based on a SF approach to the training of mentors at the Teacher Education Centre of Excellence (Special Education), Education Queensland which was delivered over a number of years.

Potentially, the concept of a mentor is counter to the SF paradigm of the person being the expert in their world, as a mentor is generally expected to bring knowledge and experience to share with their mentee. However, as the SF approach underpinned the training, it is felt that it is useful to share the structure, activities and background as this might be useful to other contexts. In addition, Insoo Kim Berg has been quoted as stating the following when asked about sharing knowledge: 'If you have knowledge or information which might be useful to the client, why wouldn't you share it?' The key for us is the invitational nature of any 'advice' where the autonomy to act on this or not lies with the mentee.

Summary of the proposal

The Teacher Education Centre of Excellence (Special Education) was seeking training in mentoring. The specific skills they wanted to be covered needed to include:

- role of a mentor
- building and sustaining the mentoring relationship
- giving feedback
- goal setting.

The focus was to build the capacity of the mentors to be more effective in their role. They initially requested one day of training but, after discussion, a total of three days was delivered in line with best practice models of mentor training.

Objectives

The training was focused on achieving the following objectives:

- shared clarity on the role of the mentor
- increased knowledge and skills on how to build and sustain an effective mentoring relationship
- increased knowledge and skills on 'coaching' approaches to setting goals and giving feedback

- a shared understanding of how to respond to difficult scenarios

- an agreed way forward in supporting mentors and mentees

- greater experience in applying practical skills of mentoring

- further in-depth training in the SF approach to mentoring

- a follow-up face-to-face opportunity to find solutions to issues encountered

- an agreed way forward in supporting mentors both this year and beyond.

Proposed measures of success

By undertaking this training, mentors will:

- be more effective in their role

- have a range of strategies to support and challenge mentees

- have an agreed approach to supporting each other and the programme beyond the initial training

- have further practice embedding the requisite mentoring skills

- gain further in-depth knowledge of the role and skills of mentoring

- have an opportunity to reflect on their current practice and identify what further support and training they require.

Methodology

From discussion with the Head of Mentoring and the Governance Committee, it was proposed that the course contain the following elements:

- role of mentor
  - » what mentoring is and isn't
  - » self-assessment
- the mentoring relationship
  - » the four stages of working with mentees

- the four strands of successful mentoring
  - » Solution Focused
  - » emotional intelligence
  - » goal-setting
  - » giving feedback
- scenarios and solutions
  - » working with Gen Y'ers
  - » working with other support systems
  - » managing expectations
- the way forward
  - » co-mentoring
  - » mentor growth plans
  - » supporting strategies.

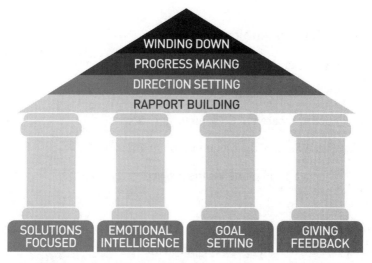

Figure 5.1: A Solutions Focused approach to mentoring

Source: Burnett (2013)

Note: This was later modified to have Solutions Focus as the underpinning foundation to the training as opposed to one of the pillars in the above model.

The Simple Model

The SF methodology is built around a framework of principles known by the acronym SIMPLE (Jackson and McKergow, 2007). The six principles of the model are as follows:

1. **Solutions** not problems.

2. **In between** — the action is in the interaction.

3. **Make** use of what's there.

4. **Possibilities** — past, present and future.

5. **Language** — simply said.

6. **Every** case is different.

The following Solution Tools (Jackson and McKergow, 2007) along with some possibly useful questions were shared to help develop a greater understanding of adopting a SF approach:

Platform (Starting point)

- Who is a customer and for what?

- Who wants something to be different?

- Who is prepared to do something?

- What would be the benefit in moving forward?

- What is a good name for the project?

Future Perfect

Life in detail…with the problem vanished:

- Miracle Question

  » What will be the first signs that let you know this transformation has happened?

  » What else? What else?

>> Who else will notice?

>> What will be the first signs they notice? What else?

Scale – building on what works

- On a scale from 1 to 10 where 10 is the Future Perfect, where are you now?

- What's helping you reach that level? What else?

- What would one step higher up the scale look like?

- What would be the first tiny signs of progress?

- What would take you one small step higher?

Counters – finding what's working

- When does the Future Perfect already happen?

- When do bits of the Future Perfect already happen?

- On a scale of 1–10, how come you are as high as you are and not lower?

- What is going well?

- What is the best you ever did at this thing?

- What's better since last time?

- How did you do that?

Affirming – noticing useful qualities, skills and resources

- What's most impressive about what has already happened?

- What impresses you about the other people involved?

- What skills, resources and qualities can be observed?

- What are the grounds for optimism?

Small actions – finding small actions

- Do more of what works:

  » small steps

  » can be taken quickly

  » starting, not stopping

  » specific and concrete

  » for the customer for change (the mentee).

- If nothing is working…stop doing what doesn't work and do something different.

A mentors SF self-assessment framework was also developed for the Teacher Education Centre of Excellence (Special Education) training.

Mentor self-assessment structure

Questioner:

- On a scale of 1–10 where are you now in relation to this?

- How come it's a [n] and not a [n–1] or [n–2]?

- What's going well?

- How did you do that?

- What else is going well? How did you do that? etc. (5 minutes)

Affirmers and Questioner:

- 'Counter Gossip' (this is what we call what the affirmers are doing) about what impresses them about the mentor and how they are tackling this situation. (2 minutes)

Questioner:

- What would a [n +1] look like?

- What would be a first small step towards that? (2 minutes)

The following SF activities were all adapted from Röhrig and Clarke (2008) to enable mentors to further examine both their own level of knowledge and experience as well as exposing them to further SF tools.

The Reflecting Telescope

- Suppose you stopped doing what isn't working, what would you be doing instead?

- What's the first sign you will notice, that tells you things are changing?

- What will be the advantages of these little changes to you?

- Who will be the first person to notice something has changed?

- How will others react if this change occurs?

- How will you know that coming here was useful?

- Suppose you were doing things differently, what would you want others to notice?

SF approach to direction setting

What's working?

Partner (this work is done in pairs) – ask them…

- What is the thing you want to be more of?

- Think of a time when you managed to do that, even if a little…

  » What did you do that helped?

  » What else? What else?

When even more is working

Now, ask your partner to suppose that next time they need to be more of the person they identified, it goes perfectly…

- What would be happening?

- What would they be doing?

- Who would be the first person to notice?

- What would they notice?

- What else? What else?

- Who else would notice? What would they notice? What else?

Affirming

Think for a moment then tell your partner…

- Two things that impress you about them.

- 'Based on what you just said, it seems to me that maybe you are a […] person.'

First signs

Partner then ask…

- What would be the first signs that you were being more […]?

- What else?

- Based on what you have said, what would be the first small step towards being more […]?

- What else?

- When can you try this?

Scenarios and solutions

Mini-coaching activity

Suggested structure:

- Establish the platform.

- Where are you on a scale of 1–10?

- What is in place that makes it [n] and not [n−1]?

- What else? What else?

- Suppose you moved to one step further on the scale. What would be a sign? Who would notice?

- What else? What else?

A SF approach to feedback

An important element to the role of mentor was that of observing a beginning teacher's lesson. Over the duration of the three years the programme was running, there were various iterations, with the version shown in Figure 5.2 being the final version.

Conclusion

This chapter has attempted to unpack some of the ingredients that are useful in being able to implement a SFSE approach to teaching and learning processes. One of the key elements we would like to draw attention to again is that, in adopting a SFSE approach, we believe that professional input should be reframed as suggestions, as opposed to recommendations, wherever possible.

We hope that the range of examples prove useful to schools wanting to adopt SF teaching and learning processes in their school.

_____ SCHOOL - LESSON OBSERVATION FORM

Date / Time:	Duration:
Mentee:	Year Gr. & Subject:
Mentor:	No. in Class:
Focus of observation:	

Mentee reflection Scale 1 – 10 where 10 is best: What are three things that went well:	Mentor reflection Scale 1- 10 where 10 is best: What are three things that went well:
What is one thing you could do differently in the next lesson as an experiment, to move you one point up the scale?	What might you suggest the mentee do differently as an experiment, to move one point up the scale?

Figure 5.2: Lesson Observation Form

References

Armstrong, T. (2012) *Neurodiversity in the Classroom: Strength-Based Strategies to Help Students with Special Needs Succeed in School and Life.* ASCD Publications.

Burnett, N. (2013) 'A Solutions Focused approach to mentoring.' Training programme developed for The Teacher Education Centre of Excellence: Special Education (TECESE). Available at https://teach.qld.gov.au/get-supported/teces/tece-special-education (accessed 19 December 2018).

Jackson, P.Z. and McKergow, M. (2007) *The Solutions Focus*. Cheltenham: Solutions Books.

Kozik, P.L. (2008) 'Examining the effects of appreciative inquiry on IEP meetings and transition planning (doctoral dissertation).' Available at http://appreciativeinquiry.case. edu/uploads/PL%20Kozik%20Dissertation%208-08.pdf.

Mahlberg, K. and Sjoblom, M. (2004) *Solution Focused Education*. Stockholm: Mareld.

National Disability Authority (2012) 'So what is person-centred planning?' Available at http://nda.ie/Good-practice/Guidelines/Guidelines-on-Person-Centered-Planning/ Guidelines-on-Person-Centred-Planning-format-versions/2-What-is-Person-Centred-Planning- (accessed 2/10/2018).

Röhrig, P. and Clarke, J. (eds) (2008) *57 SF Activities for Facilitators and Consultants: Putting Solutions Focus into Action*. Cheltenham: Solutions Books.

Chapter 6

SOLUTIONS FOCUSED SPECIAL EDUCATION BEHAVIOUR SUPPORT

Nick Burnett, Dr Geoffrey James and Lee Shilts ─────────

Introduction

Whatever the cause of the behaviour is, whether it is a learned difficulty, a problem of motivation, a psycho-educational issue, or a social and family functioning issue, we usually begin exploring what behaviour support should be provided using the following approach:

1. Identify what the problem of the child, parent, peer, teacher or the school is.

2. Look at the historical trend, trauma, bad learning habit, or even bad parenting that may have contributed to the current problem.

3. Put them into neat, easily understandable categories of problems. (This task is carried out by experts who are trained to identify what the problem is and how to classify it.)

4. Find a matching solution or remedy for each category of problems.

5. The expert prescribes, suggests, or recommends detailed steps to a solution so that a parent or teacher could carry out the steps to find a solution.

It is easy to see why this kind of approach could generate disagreement from students, teachers, parents and/or administrators who might have their own ideas of what the problem is and what solutions might work better. If they do not downright disagree openly with the suggested solutions, they might have their own ideas on what might work better.

At best, when forced to carry out something they do not believe might work, most reasonable people tend to make a half-hearted, reluctant attempt to carry out the solution identified by someone else.

We believe that since the problem occurs in classrooms, wherever possible, solutions should also be created in the classroom.

This chapter will explore a number of Solutions Focused (SF) approaches to supporting behaviour. These will be explored in two major sections with Lee Shilts and Nick Burnett co-authoring the first section 'Working on What Works (WoWW) and POSITIVE', and Geoffrey James then sharing his 1:1 behaviour support coaching with students and the development of a whole-school approach using SF Coaching. These will be quite different in style as appropriate to the author(s):

1. Working on What Works (WoWW) – a behaviour support approach co-developed by Lee Shilts with Insoo Kim Berg.

    From exploring WoWW, a possible way forward for those working with the most complex of students with special educational needs, called POSITIVE, will be suggested.

2. SF Coaching – this will explore 1:1 work and also the development of a whole-school approach.

Both the WoWW and SF Coaching sections will start with a case study before moving on to an explanation of the background, rationale and process for each of the approaches.

Working on What Works (WoWW) and POSITIVE
Lee Shilts and Nick Burnett

CASE STUDY 1: USING WOWW IN THE CLASSROOM

Michelle Washburn-Busk

Michelle is a graduate student at Kansas State at the PhD and Masters levels. She, along with their lead faculty, Amber Vennum, began using WoWW in the Manhattan, KS school district as a research project. Working from the same premise as Insoo Kim Berg and Lee Shilts' original work, they incorporated the WoWW intervention into secondary schools. The graduate students served as the coaches. Prior to this, Lee Shilts had gone to Kansas State and done two days of training with the students and Amber on WoWW.

The story

In a classroom where I was doing WoWW, there was a student who had a reputation as a trouble-maker. Whenever I'd walk into the break room to have lunch with the teachers to talk about the progress in their classrooms, the teachers were often swapping 'horror stories' about this student, sharing experiences they'd had of trying to 'get through to him' and failing, and remarking about how his whole family was troubled because they'd had issues with his older brother, too.

When observing the maths period of this boy, I saw him making bids for the teacher's attention, admittedly disruptive bids such as calling out without raising his hand, trying to make other students laugh or being distracting by combing his hair randomly or rocking in his chair. I noticed that his teacher had a pretty low threshold at this point for this sort of distracting, and sometimes disrespectful, behaviour. Multiple days in a row when I observed I saw this student do something mildly disruptive and then immediately get sent out to the hall for the *remainder* of the class period.

On one occasion, I went out to the hall to talk to this student. He seemed to feel very dejected, and I asked him what was going on for him that day. He didn't say much back, then I told him that I felt like he was a very important addition to the classroom, and that it was sad when he was asked to leave for the whole period because I felt like he had so much good to add. In the next few class periods I observed, I gave this student multiple compliments for participating in class – even disruptively. I commented on his desire to be engaged, and I told him that I recognised he was really trying. I commented on specific ways I'd seen him help others in class learn from his excellent questions and comments about the maths lessons. I also commented on his ability to focus on his assignments when he was asked.

Granted, his disruptive behaviour did not immediately stop because of these compliments, but I started to notice a shift in him: he *was* trying harder in class – participating more, distracting others less, talking to his classmates in a more collaborative way, and showing more respect to his teacher. The most important shift occurred when I talked to his teacher and said 'I wonder how you could send a message to this student about not tolerating disrespect in a way that still shows him that you *want* him in your class?' The teacher thought long and hard about it and said 'I guess when I send him out in the hall he probably doesn't feel like he belongs.' After that, the teacher sent him out gradually less and less. He began to invite him back into class sooner after sending him out, and he would take time to talk to him in the hallway in a very real way.

The small interactions I had with this student and his teacher sent a very powerful message to this student – it sent the message that he was *wanted,* and that he didn't need to try to reject others before they rejected him. He began to take more risks to try to belong, rather than distance himself from people who could hurt him. I think he began to view this maths teacher as a trusted adult who understood him more deeply, and I think the maths teacher began to realise the power of a paradigm shift toward seeing the positive that helped him 'get through' to this student.

Background, rationale and process for WoWW

Solutions are part of a different language game that may be unconnected to the problems language game. The lack of connection between problems-focused and solution focused language games is central to the practice of solution focused therapy.

This quote by de Shazer (1988) captures the essence of what WoWW is intended to do in the day-to-day work in the classroom with the participants involved (teachers, students, parents, administrators and so forth). Once this is in place, the classroom environment should take on a whole new 'language game' that promotes positive interactions and observations.

WoWW originated in Florida from a discussion about an individual pupil being taught by Lee's wife. A solution focused discussion between Lee, his wife and Insoo Kim Berg led to an observation by Lee and Berg in the classroom and positive feedback to the child whose behaviour was causing concern (highlighting positives from observation, for example, concentrating on work, being polite).

Berg, along with Lee, developed the WoWW approach from this initial intervention, incorporating more solution focused elements in the process. Berg and Lee state that their model emerged through repeated observations of what worked and what did not work, removing the elements that did not work and developing those that did.

WoWW focuses on the solution focused principles of:

- looking for exceptions to problem situations (times when the problem situation is less problematic, or the problem does not exist)

- working on what already is working (maintaining and building on existing good practice)

- believing that change is constant and inevitable and that professionals should always be looking for small, positive changes which can be built on to bring about bigger change – the 'snowball effect'.

WoWW is described as a practical tool to help solve everyday problems in the classroom. WoWW also recognised that the classroom problems should be solved within the classroom, not isolated away from the natural setting of the problem to be dealt with by someone other than the student's teacher. It aims to build positive relationships between the teacher and pupils through collaborative goal setting and team working.

Berg and Shilts (2005) outline the process of the WoWW programme, which has three key stages:

- Stage 1: Observation (three weeks) (Kelly, Kim and Franklin, 2008). The WoWW 'coach' (someone external to the classroom) observes the class looking for positive things to feedback to the pupils and class teacher (CT). Following the observation, each pupil is given individual feedback about one positive thing the observer noticed. They state that time should be taken to give the CT his/her feedback after class.

- Stage 2: The WoWW coaches facilitate discussion to set collaborative (teacher and pupil) classroom goals (around Weeks 4 or 5). These goals are then scaled by the pupils and CT on a scale from 1 to 10. The rating provided should take into consideration the class as a whole, rather than individual pupils. The class is asked what it would take to move one point up the scale.

- Stage 3: Regular scaling of classroom success and amplifying. The goals set in Stage 2 are the focus of observer feedback during the remaining WoWW sessions. Between sessions, the CT should work with the pupils to scale themselves daily to amplify change (by highlighting progress to be built upon).

Major tenets and assumptions of WoWW

- Theory of No Theory.

- If it is not broken, don't fix it.

- If it works, do more of it.

- If it doesn't work, don't do it again. Do something different.

- Change is constant; change is inevitable.

- The future is negotiated and created.

- There is no direct connection between problems and solutions.

- No problem happens all the time.

- Hold students accountable for solutions.

- Questions shape the answers.

Key elements
Exceptions to problems

Capitalising on these exceptions that everybody has is a very creative and efficient way for children to discover their own resourcefulness and small successes. For example, in order to be called 'truant', a child must come to school from time to time.

Acquiring new skills takes time and repeated effort at mastery of skills. Exceptions, in contrast, are knowledge and skills the child already knows how to do. Getting the child to repeat what he knows how to do is much more effective and efficient.

Classroom success scales

To design a scale that is most useful, everyone must agree on the end points. It is important to describe the presence of the preferred behaviour and experience in as much detail as possible and to keep working on describing the '10' of their end point as the absence of something (i.e. when there is no problem).

Compliments, compliments and more compliments

Compliments are the cornerstone of SF practice.

Compliments can be organised into three different categories: direct compliments, indirect compliments and self-compliments. An indirect compliment might be suggested by the following question:

Coach: 'Suppose I ask your best friend, what would he say about how you managed to get to school on time today?'

The rule is always listening for *what* is important to the student and following up on their thinking.

Other elements to the WoWW approach

The WoWW approach encourages teachers to collaborate with the child to set goals, solicit their ideas for solutions and look for small successes to build on.

Goal setting: WoWW is a set of goal-driven activities. We begin with a set of goals and then devise a plan to achieve them. WoWW also means we have a vision of where we want to be at the end of the school year.

The WoWW programme views learning activities differently; all learning should be driven by students, not by teachers, with the following elements being important as to how WoWW can be supported by teachers:

- Curiosity. When using the scaling question, what should you do when the student's answer is very low on the scale? Become curious about how it is that this child is standing in front of you and seems to be functioning reasonably well. Be creative, innovative and, most of all, use your and the child's imagination, since all children have plenty of imagination.

- Selective attention – watching and listening for small successes. Traditional classroom behaviour management has been focused on watching and paying attention to potential troublesome spots or behaviour that could possibly get out of control. However, we are not in the business of managing children's behaviour, we are in the business of educating children. Ask about how he *stops* this disruptive behaviour. Eventually, he will become curious about his own behaviour and how he makes it more positive.

- Letters and notes to students. Recognise, in concrete ways, times when the student has been engaged in behaviours that are wanted.

- Letters and phone calls to parents. Rather than talking about the child's problems, difficult situations, or what the school would like parents to do differently, always begin your conversations with parents by making some compliments about their children. Again, the more factual and behavioural the compliment, the more encouraged the parents will become. If at all possible, 'positive blame' the parent, giving them the credit for what the child is doing well.

Possible implications for special education

WoWW is a critical realist development: observation of a phenomenon (empirical level); evidence from looking at what was happening in the groups, 'what's working' and 'what's not working' (actual level); tentative description of mechanisms, for example social construction of change, change as a constant, etc. (real level).

It is doing more than skills development because it explicitly includes the social, 'becoming-someone' aspect of children's learning and growth. This underpins our belief that since the problem occurs in the classroom, solutions should be created there.

WoWW has been the subject of a number of papers. Brown, Powell and Clark (2012) reflect that the WoWW approach is flexible and can be adapted to suit pupils of all ages and abilities. They also reference the work of Kelly and Bluestone-Miller (2009) who describe evaluation of the approach being used with Kindergarten through to eighth-grade pupils.

Whilst it undoubtedly has great flexibility and adaptability, the question is whether it can meet the needs of the most complex students in special education who may have combinations, or all, of the following, and more, challenges:

- language

  » receptive

  » expressive

- cognitive delay

- Autistic Spectrum Disorder/Oppositional Defiant Disorder

- violent and aggressive behaviour

  » towards self

  » towards others.

Using the major tenets of WoWW as a starting point:

- *Theory of No Theory* – we would suggest that this is an important basis to SFSE behaviour support, although the proviso is that some knowledge of the difficulties faced can offer some suggestions as to ways of working.

- *If it is not broken, don't fix it* – perhaps this can be a useful reminder about not changing things that are working, although in the field of special education, what works one day or hour may not work the next.

- *If it works, do more of it* – increasing the focus on the times when things are going well is an important approach in all situations.

- *If it doesn't work, don't do it again. Do something different* – there is a potential issue with this tenet as for many students with challenging behaviour within special education there is a need to try things for an agreed timescale to see if they are going to be the right approach. The need to try things for a short period of time and reassess is important.

- *Change is constant; change is inevitable* – an important tenet as it is about hope in the future that things are going to change and how we can notice the positive change and use this to impact positively.

- *The future is negotiated and created* – yes, although this may not be directly with the student if they have significant language and cognitive issues. Ultimately, the student will let us know if the options being taken are the correct ones by their behaviour.

- *There is no direct connection between problems and solutions* – whilst this is important to be aware of, in special education some knowledge of the difficulties faced can offer some suggestions as to ways of working.

- *No problem happens all the time* – this is a really important tenet even with the most complex students in special education. Our focus has to be better at identifying when the problem is not occurring.

- *Hold students accountable for solutions* – this tenet is a challenge to accept with all students within special education although it should be strived for as much as possible. All those supporting the students must be accountable for helping find solutions as opposed to problems.

- *Questions shape the answers* – the language we use, as always with a Solution Focused approach, is crucial, and these questions may well be what we use with parents and staff as well as those we use with students, where possible.

Whilst WoWW is a whole-class approach, there are important elements that can be used and/or adapted in relation to those working with the most complex students within special education.

So how can we move from the knowledge around WoWW, which explores an approach that has been successfully used in a number of situations in classrooms, towards an often-needed individual approach in special education?

It is suggested that using the POSITIVE tools could be useful as they blend some of the thoughts and ideas of WoWW into an individualised support approach.

POSITIVE: Solution focused tools for behaviour support

What are the POSITIVE tools?

- possibilities

- outcomes

- scaling

- identifying counters (these are anything that is useful for the situation/child)

- taking small steps

- illuminating progress

- valuing through affirming

- exceptions.

The POSITIVE tools are exactly that, *tools*. They are not a magic wand for 'solving' challenging behaviour. They are a range of strategies and approaches that can be drawn on at the relevant time when working with those who support the individuals and the individuals themselves.

Examining being POSITIVE
Possibilities

What are the possibilities that can be imagined from past, present and future expectations of both those supporting the individual with challenging behaviour and the individual being supported?

Possibilities are central to progress. Without a clear picture of what is a preferred future it is difficult to bring about the required changes. What is happening in the present to celebrate and build on? When have there been successes in the past to draw on?

Exploring all of these possibilities with both those supporting the individual and, importantly where possible, the individual, can help bring about a more POSITIVE approach to supporting the individual.

Outcomes

How is progress going to be measured and by whom?

Having clarity regarding outcomes is important to review success. Agreed outcomes on what we want to see, as opposed to what we don't want to see, help clarify the expectations and measures of success for those supporting the individual and the individual themselves.

Scaling

Identifying a range of ways to use one of the most important SF tools in examining the current situation and ways to measure progress.

The use of scaling is a really useful approach for both those supporting the individual and the individual themselves. It can be used to help with the next tool, identifying counters, as well as progress towards agreed outcomes.

Identifying counters

Identifying the possible counters of both the individual who displays challenging behaviour and those who support them can be important in moving things forward.

This will often be used in conjunction with a number of the other tools. After using scaling to identify, for example, how well we are supporting the student with challenging behaviour, examination of why the number is n as opposed to n−1 can help identify counters that those supporting the individual have, and that can be used more. It can also be used to identify the counters that the individuals have available to help themselves.

Taking small steps

Identifying and taking the first small steps towards a jointly preferred outcome can help bring a feeling of progress to even the most difficult situations. Often those supporting individuals who display challenging behaviour are looking for major changes. Whilst this may be the final goal of the work in supporting the individual, to look for major changes is often unhelpful and unrealistic and so all can become disheartened. Identifying and taking small steps in the preferred direction can help all involved feel more positive and wish to continue in identifying ways forward.

Illuminating progress

Illuminating what has gone well and what progress has been made can help identify a possible way forward and also assist with a more positive view of supporting the individual. Identifying times when progress was made can help clarify strategies that may be useful in assisting with further progress.

Valuing through affirming

This means valuing through affirming the quality, resource or skill that the individual, and those who support them, bring to the situation. The importance of affirming is often unrecognised but being able to recognise the skills, qualities and strengths that were, and are, being displayed, helps people feel more positive to the individual and situation in which they find themselves.

Exceptions

This is about finding the exceptions when the individual is displaying the preferred behaviours and building on these successes. No individual is always behaving in a challenging and inappropriate way. The challenge is for those working with the individual to identify the exceptions and build on what is happening at that time to try and have more 'exceptions'.

Additional thoughts

The WoWW idea of having external people to the class come and observe and share the successes they see has much to offer in our view as it gives a different perspective. Whilst this may not be important to the individual being supported, it can have a lot to offer to supporting staff and parents as to possible ways of building on successes and moving forward.

CASE STUDY 2: **SF COACHING – WORKING 1:1 TO SUPPORT STUDENT BEHAVIOUR**

Dr Geoffrey James

Jen was 14 when I met her for the first time. She had been permanently excluded from two schools and was just starting off at her new, third, school. This was was when I was on secondment to the Child and Adolescent Mental Health Service from my main job as a local authority specialist behaviour support teacher and the referral had come via CAMHS where Jen had an open case file with multiple diagnoses. (Child and Adolescent Mental Health Services (CAMHS) provide comprehensive services for children and adolescents experiencing mental health problems.) My role was to build the bridge between CAMHS and the Local Education Authority, supporting her into her new school. I had worked with the school Special Educational Needs and Disability Co-ordinator (SENDCo) before, so she knew that I would be working with Jen using the Solutions Focused Coaching approach.

I arranged to meet Jen and the SENDCo at the school office, to be shown to a meeting room.

When we were settled, the SENDCo left us. Jen and I got to work.

'Thanks for coming to meet me today. I'm Geoff. My job is to work with students who are making changes in school and coming here is a big change for you, I guess. What would you like me to call you?'

'Jen.'

'OK, Jen. We've got half an hour. Is that OK with you?'

'Yes.'

'I'd like to ask you a question. What would be useful to you, for us to be working on today?'

'I don't know.'

'Hmmm. That's a useful answer...tells me I need to ask you something a bit different. Suppose you *did* know what might be useful to you today, what might that be?

'My behaviour?'

'So if we did some work on "my behaviour" that would that be useful to you, would it?'

'Yes.'

'That's our project then. We'll hang that up for a bit because I'd like to ask you about something else. What's your best thing... What do you like doing best?'

And she told me.

I reflected what she said back to her from time to time and asked her for more details of her story: 'What else?' or 'So what is about *you*, that you could do that?'

And she told me about her strengths and resources.

From time to time I complimented her and checked to see if I'd got it right. She told me about going to the city with her friends. 'It seems to me that you're a person who gets on with your friends. Is that right?'

I asked her what other people might notice about her.

I asked her 'What else?'

After about 20 minutes of this problem-free talk, I thanked her for the conversation and said we'd move back to the 'My behaviour' project.

I drew a horizontal scale on a blank page of the notepad I was using to keep track of our conversation, with one on the left and ten on the right hand. I gave her the notepad and pen.

'If this is your "My behaviour" scale, ten is "My behaviour" being good enough for things to go well for you in your new school and one is the opposite. Where would you put yourself now?'

'Seven?'

'So what tells you you're at seven?'

And she told me.

'Suppose we met next week and I asked you where you are on your scale, where do you hope you might be? What's your best hope for next week?'

'Eight?'

'Hmmm…eight. OK. We're just about finished for today. There are two things left. One is to give you a job to do, the other is compliments. First, your job – it's to look out for things going well for you. OK? So what's your job?'

'Notice what's going well?'

'That's it, exactly. Now for compliments, my compliment to you and yours to yourself. Who do you want to go first?'

We finished on time, 30 minutes exactly. We agreed to meet at a different time the next week, to make sure she didn't miss the same class every time.

A week later, she was ready to tell me how she'd got on.

'I said I'd ask you to tell me about what's going well. So…what's going well?'

'I'm at eight now!'

'At eight now – what tells you that?'

And:

'What would your teachers be noticing that would tell them you're at eight?'

And:

'What's your best hope for next week?'

We met weekly for a month and reviewed the work after the fifth meeting. Jen decided she wasn't quite done with our work and said she'd like to meet again. We met over another month and then intermittently, when she got in touch with me through the SENDCo. She stayed in school, she never had time off and took her GCSEs there.

It's unusual for a teenager who has been permanently excluded twice to complete their education in a mainstream school. The fact that she did says something about both herself and her school. They didn't give up.

CASE STUDY 3: **SF COACHING AS A WHOLE-SCHOOL PRACTICE**

In the summer of 2016, I ran a two-day SF Coaching training course in Lincolnshire, as part of the county's strategy to eliminate exclusion. Until recently, the Lincolnshire County Council region had the highest exclusion rate in England.

> 'Lincolnshire Ladder of Behavioural Intervention (LLBI) is designed to support schools in achieving zero exclusion; the full inclusion of our most vulnerable pupils through early, evidence-based intervention and, if necessary, collaboration between settings.' (Lincolnshire County Council Lincolnshire Learning Partnership, 2015)

The 'Ladder' states that it is based in the SF approach. I have been involved in bringing SF practice, with SF Coaching, SF pastoral support planning and SF school policy into action.

Two senior staff from a city secondary school, Lincoln Christ's Hospital School (Lincolnshire has grammar and secondary schools), came to a training session in the last week of the summer term. My course has real SF practice exercises as a core element and during the first day they checked out with me that it was OK if they shortened the exercises, because they had a lot to talk to each other about. It transpired that no sooner had they got hold of the shift in thinking, with the ideas underpinning SF Coaching that the child is the expert, that they can be seen as doing their best even when it didn't seem like it, that shifting from a focus on the problem to the focus on solutions strengthened the child's hopeful nature and their relationship and engagement in the work, than they realised a previously overlooked fact. They had a school policy on exclusion when what they needed was an inclusion policy. This school was the highest excluder in the highest excluding county, because they had an exclusion policy and they followed it to the letter!

I contacted them near the autumn half-term. Over the summer holiday they had scrapped the exclusion policy and written an inclusion policy, which they agreed to put on my website: thesolutionsfocusedcoach.com.

SF Coaching was built into the school's pastoral repertoire, not just for children labelled with the 'behaviour' tag, but for all children struggling in school. They sent other members of their team for training, briefed the staff in school and recorded a major drop in both permanent and fixed-term exclusion. Eighteen months later, SF Coaching is embedded in the school. Students who go to the Turnaround Centre in school for support are subsequently remaining in class, without the need for further coaching. Consequences for rule-breaking are still in place for routine classroom management purposes. However, where a student makes more serious errors in behaviour which impinge on their engagement and learning, encompassing both the obvious, outgoing, challenging kind of behaviour and the more private, withdrawn and disengaged kind, they are entitled to SF Coaching, a fully educational process drawing on Inquiry pedagogy and carried out by school staff in school hours.

Across the county, exclusion rates have fallen, and progress is being sustained.

Background, rationale and process

I have been using SF coaching since 2001 to support children struggling in school. As a specialist teacher working for a local authority Children's Services in England, I had to be pigeonholed, because services demand structure for planning purposes.

Specialist teachers operate down two channels, splitting Learning Support from Behaviour Support. In 1995 I started teaching science in an all-age, residential, special school for children with emotional and behaviour difficulties. In 1998 I moved on to teach in an 11–16 Pupil Referral Unit with children who had been excluded from school. I was also assigned as a specialist teacher to schools to help them out when they needed an expert. I was doing Behaviour Support.

As a behaviour expert, for three years before I discovered SF practice, I was expected to act as an expert. Mainstream, special schools and what we call 'alternative provision' had done everything that was written down in their school behaviour policy statements to get children to toe the line and then I was called in. Why did they expect me to know more than they did, with their accumulated wisdom and personal knowledge of the children who struggled? If only they knew the truth. They had already been looking for causes and triggers of this or that behaviour, for why children did no work, or caused a fuss in a particular class, or always seemed to be demanding attention. All I could do was more of the same, floundering about in the hope of finding something that might make a difference.

When I met the SF approach, in a one-day course in Solution Focused Brief Therapy (SFBT) presented by Harvey Ratner from Brief, London, I realised that here was a structured way of working that broke all the rules of expertise. Working within an Educational Psychology Service I was required to provide an intervention designed to respond to an identified deficit. It is what we did, strictly following the medical model. I would receive a referral to work with a child whose behaviour was seen as the problem and was expected to solve it, which I duly did.

Or appeared to do. But the structure of SF practice told me to put the detailed report of deficits to one side and work with the person in the room, as a successful, resourceful being, hoping for a better future.

SF Coaching is the term I use to describe my work in and with schools, training school staff and doing direct work myself. My long-term project is to increase the capacity of schools to support children, their parents and carers and themselves. I call the work 'Coaching' rather than 'therapy', as do others developing SFBT in different strands, all of which link directly back to the original ideas of Steve de Shazar, Insoo Kim Berg and their co-workers.

In my development of SF Coaching for schools, I have clear principles to follow and communicate to SF Coaching trainees:

- *Talking to the Elephant.* New scientific findings show that people communicate emotionally first and follow this up with cognitive checking. This is rooted in the various transmission speeds of different neurones and the phenomenon of interoception. The brain receives signals from within itself and the body as it responds to events outside, like threat or danger, and puts these together with memories and experience to predict what might happen next. The Elephant is the powerful and rapid reactor which sets the direction of travel for the cognitive rider. Approaching Jen knowing that she is successful, resourceful and hopeful sets up the possibility that we can explore the problem-free world and, once on the path to success, keep going in that direction.

- *Power and positioning.* Working with Jen, I am careful to maintain her sense of agency by monitoring our relative positioning. Her story has pride of place, her experience is the only topic of importance. The 'preferred future' question at the start which sets up the project is minimalised, with attention rapidly shifting to her successes and achievements in life. The work is informed by her goal but not directed by it, because her best hope is her possession; she can modify it as she wishes and probably will as things change around her. It is flexible, not rigid. And most importantly what is happening in the moment is what we're paying attention to. Remembered successes are happening in the moment of remembering. The recognition of strengths and resources is in the moment of realisation. SF conversation is a mindful act and mindfulness allows for the emergence of the sense of flow and the happiness that it brings with it. I say more about this in my 2016 book (James, 2016).

- *I aim to be invisible*, giving no advice and centring my expertise on being the best SF Coach I can be, in the room with the client. I ask the most ordinary of questions, reflecting her own use of language. At close of coaching I ask the client 'Who has made the change, who has made this happen?' I have to be confident that they can answer 'Well, I guess it must be me.' For that I have to know that I have been scrupulous in maintaining fidelity to the principles of SF practice.

- *Scaling is similarly power sensitive.* The scale is a good way to generate description, to fill out the details of the story of hope and hopeful change. It's not there to force change to happen (solutions focused, not solution forced).

My work with Lincolnshire County Council has been in line with my direction of travel since 1998 when I started working on my PhD. My thesis title is 'Finding a pedagogy'. (My full thesis is available at thesolutionsfocusedcoach.com.) My research was about finding an alternative to the psychologically based behaviourist reward-and-punishment approach used by most schools in the UK with an educational way of working with children in distress that could be taken up by schools as part of their routine teaching and leaning work.

SF practice is a form of pedagogy known as Inquiry, aligned with Carl Rogers' person-centred approach in which the teacher facilitates learning rather than directing it, as described in his 1969 book *Freedom to Learn*, revised in 1983 (Rogers, 1983). The subsequent development of SF Coaching, following initial two-day training, has been in the hands of the school community. Having made such a dramatic initial step-change, the school is moving steadily towards its goal of full inclusion of all children, at its own pace within its own resources.

A benefit to staff is that where previously they would do what they could, following the procedures of stepped punishment, but come to a dead end, where exclusion appeared to be the last resort, now they have an open-ended way of working with SF Coaching. Being non-diagnostic and strength-focused means they share the processor learning with the student, walking with them along the path of change. This matches the natural human tendency to co-operate in kindness and removes the stress of trying to be the universal expert in other people's problems. There is potential here for a school to become a SF community, where people at all levels take the SF approach in planning and achieving success, guided by their own sense of competency and hope.

Next step

My next step is to build external research into the outcomes of training programmes I am providing in 2018 for groups of schools. I am in conversation with Professor Jonathan Glazzard of Leeds Beckett University, Carnegie School of Education, to take this forward, hoping to report our findings in 2019.

Conclusion
Nick Burnett, Lee Shilts and Geoffrey James

We hold that there is only one solution focused approach within the SF paradigm, in the same way that there is only one hypothesis-testing approach within the positivist paradigm. This is illustrated by the way that Insoo Kim Berg and Lee Shilts approached their development of WoWW. The POSITIVE tools are suggested as being useful in assisting in the support of individuals who display challenging behaviour at an organisation and/or individual level.

We also acknowledge that there is a 'danger' in calling the tools POSITIVE because of the always-present power of the positivist paradigm: 'Oh, SF is just about being positive!'

Geoffrey James similarly points out the essential connection of SF Coaching in schools with the original form of SFBT.

SF is more than being positive. It's about matching hopes with the changes people are experiencing. A clear example was the SF training for workers in an alcohol and substance misuse service provided by one of the authors, whose homeless clients could report nothing positive in their lives and needed SF clarity to notice what they were doing in coping, with things being so bad and not getting worse, with coming into the service centre to talk at all, even after missed appointments. Insoo Kim Berg's range of 'wow' comments, from the quietest murmur to smiling exclamation in matching her client's description of success, stands on the same principle.

Whilst there is much about behaviour support that has no difference whether the behaviour occurs in mainstream or special education, and WoWW and SF Coaching have much to offer in both settings, there are some students who have an increased level of complexity where an individualised approach is needed. The mindful and respectful nature of SF practice aligns the SF conversation with the people in the room, without making assumptions about their level of language and communication. Dr Geoffrey James reports several instances where the client, a child in special school, barely spoke at all, yet the work went ahead on the basis that everyone was doing their best in the best way they knew. And sometimes the quietest conversation with space and time for silences gives a unique opportunity to hear and listen to the true voice of the child.

We will finish this chapter with a description of an interesting approach to dealing with incidents that unfortunately end up having to be dealt with by the legal system.

Solution focused judging

Whilst we hope that these approaches reduce the conflict between child and system, currently a disproportionate number of individuals with, often undiagnosed, special needs frequently find themselves in the justice system. It was heartening to hear of an approach developed in Australia and being deliberately practised in Wellington, New Zealand called the Solution Focused Judging Bench Book (AIJA, 2017).

The Bench Book acknowledges that judging in problem-solving programmes involves a number of considerations, such as the need to promote positive behavioural change and the wellbeing of participants; the need to hold participants accountable for their actions; the need to maintain the integrity of the court programme and the wellbeing of the court team; and the obligation to apply relevant provisions of statute law and the common law. It recognises that sometimes there is tension between two or more of these considerations. The Bench Book takes an optimistic, 'glass half full' approach to participants in problem-solving court programmes. It sees them not only as citizens who have offended and who have offending-related problems, or who otherwise have problems with the law, but also as human beings who have strengths and insight into, and possible solutions for, their problems.

As we said, we hope that this is not something those with special needs who display behaviour that challenges end up facing, but if they do we hope it is dealt with through this approach.

References

AIJA (2017) Solution Focused Judging Bench Book. Available at https://aija.org.au/wp-content/uploads/2017/07/Solution-Focused-Judging-Bench-Book.pdf (accessed 2/10/2018).

Berg, I.K. and Shilts, L. (2005) *Classroom Solutions: WOWW Coaching*. Milwaukee, WI: BFTC Press.

Brown, E.L., Powell, E. and Clark, A. (2012) 'Working on What Works: working with teachers to improve classroom behaviour and relationships.' *Educational Psychology in Practice*, 28(1), 19–30. Doi: 10.1080/02667363.2011.639347.

de Shazer, S. (1988) *Investigating Solutions in Brief Therapy*. New York: W.W. Norton and Company.

James, G. (2016) *Transforming Behaviour in the Classroom: A Solution Focused Guide for New Teachers*. London and New York: Sage.

Kelly, M.S. and Bluestone-Miller, R. (2009) 'Working on What Works (WOWW): coaching teachers to do more of what's working.' *Children and Schools*, 31(1), 35–38.

Kelly, M.S., Kim, J.S. and Franklin, C. (2008) *Solution focused Brief Therapy in Schools: A 360-degree View of Research and Practice*. New York: Oxford University Press.

Lincolnshire County Council Lincolnshire Learning Partnership (2015) 'Inclusive Lincolnshire.' Available at https://lincolnshire.moderngov.co.uk/documents/s12917/6.0%20Appendix%20A%20Inclusive%20Lincolnshire%20Strategy%20v2.2%20-%20Post%20LLPB.pdf (accessed 17/10/2018).

Rogers, C. (1983) *Freedom to Learn for the 80s, 2nd Revised Edition*. Columbus, OH: Merrill

Chapter 7

SOLUTION FOCUSED SPECIAL EDUCATION PARTNERSHIPS WITH FAMILY AND COMMUNITY

Nick Burnett and Michael Doneman

Introduction

The focus of this chapter is sharing and exploring a range of examples in relation to partnerships with family and community, as we believe these are important elements within the overall implementation of Solutions Focused Special Education (SFSE).

The family element is, we hope, clear as to its importance. Whilst the community may seem less clear cut, we believe effective SFSE involves the community to the extent that it has benefit to the individual student, and many students within special education have involvement with a range of other services and professionals, many of which would benefit from adopting a Solutions Focused (SF) approach.

We will also share examples from the community that explore possibilities beyond school as some students will require a range of ongoing levels of support beyond compulsory schooling.

Reflecting on one of the co-authors' time as a Special School Principal in the UK, and echoing the sentiments of Ben Furman in his foreword to the book *Solution Focused Education* (Mahlberg and Sjoblom, 2004), we believe that we need to explore how we can co-operate, collaborate and co-create better with parents and the community to enable the best possible outcomes and provision for the individual with special needs. This is not to suggest that many schools are not doing a good

job in this area, more to reflect on what would make it even better. Additionally, although many special schools already have good links with the community, we also believe there is much more on offer for the community and the student.

In relation to partnerships with parents, this chapter will draw on examples from Mahlberg and Sjoblom (2004) from their own experiences in running a special school. Additionally, we will reflect on the excellent work on personalising education by Helen Sanderson and Associates, which appears to be very SF in nature, even though not explicitly so. In recognising this, we will be offering some suggestions as to how the suggested processes contained within the personalising education work could be even more SF.

In terms of community examples, we will explore two particular case studies. One is from one of the co-authors, where the case study comes from a community business environment where a person-centred solution focused approach to business planning has been implemented. The other is exploring a range of person-centred approaches implemented by Kingwood Community who support individuals with Autism Spectrum Disorder (ASD) through a range of projects which, whilst not explicitly SF, have a strong connection to this way of operating.

We will then explore external services who have explicitly adopted a SF approach to their work, namely the National Society for the Prevention of Cruelty to Children (NSPCC) in their face-to-face work with children and young people. We would want to recognise that this service is not exclusive to those with special needs and not all individuals with special needs are going to access this service. However, it is our experience that, for a range of reasons, there are many individuals with special needs who may need to access these support services or similar support services at some stage, and the approaches could have something to offer other support services.

Partnerships with parents and family

Ben Furman (2006) identifies that in solution focused work, we never blame the parents, regardless of their shortcomings. Instead we regard them as resources, people who in one way or another can contribute to solutions for their children. We would extend this to all family members including friends of the individual with special needs.

We will start by exploring some general thinking and questions around partnerships with parents before moving to some specific case studies as examples.

Parents as partners

Engaging with parents as partners is an important element of creating a successful SFSE environment. Ultimately, all those working in special education want children and young people to achieve, and the importance of parents in this partnership is supported in the following quote by Wolfendale: 'Involving parents and carers in education increases children's achievement' (1997, p.41).

For the sake of brevity we will use the term 'parent' to mean anyone with a responsibility for the individual with special needs including, but not limited to, carers and advocates.

In any restorative process, parents will often have an important role to play and we will start this section exploring some questions to stimulate thinking about best practice in relation to parents as partners. We will then move on to what else may need to be considered when working restoratively with parents of individuals with special needs.

Many settings and education departments have a range of questionnaires in place to measure parental satisfaction, but we would suggest that an important element missing in the assessment of a school's success is whether or not it treats the parents mainly as consumers rather than an active partner in the process. In reflecting back on one of the authors' time as a principal, it would have to be acknowledged that often when we said we were engaging with parents, we were actually playing the role of telling them what they needed to do and what we were doing, rather than explicitly engaging with them.

When settings and families work together, individuals have a far better chance of being successful in school, and successful in life as well. It is suggested that there are three Rs to effective partnerships (Williams, 2015):

- respect

- responsibility

- relationships.

The following section draws largely on the excellent blog by Patricia Williams on 'How do we build effective school–parent partnerships?' (2015) but broadens the scope to include any setting that is supporting individuals with special needs.

Respect

In looking to build respect, both the parent and those in the setting should be seen to be valued, trusted and respected. The needs of the individual come first and the individual's needs form the basis of all interactions. Both recognise that the family perspective is invaluable in providing insight and information as to what an individual needs to be successful. The parents are full partners in the decision-making process because their information is so important. There is an open-door policy at the setting. This means that there is a climate that welcomes parents and that expresses concern for their needs – the parent's needs as well as the child's needs. There is also what we call the 'recognition of limits'. Parents have limits, they have other responsibilities as well, so settings provide access to services, supports, resources and meetings at times and places that work for their parents. At the core of respect there's the underlying belief that both staff in the setting and the parent really want what's best for the individual.

Now we shall move to the second R, that of responsibility.

Responsibility

Neither the setting nor the parent blames the other for what's not working but instead they both claim responsibility for success. This means that setting staff and parents both have the responsibility to stay connected with each other. Parents need to educate the setting staff about their child. They need to share their journey with that child and staff must take responsibility for doing the same with the family. Communication needs to be regular, ongoing, two-way (including feedback) and meaningful. In other words, successful and responsible partnerships accept the need to stay informed. Responsibility means staying connected and staying informed. This is a mutual responsibility.

With respect and responsibility there is the opportunity to build meaningful relationships, the third R in successful setting–parent partnerships.

Relationships

Effective relationships build trust and trust sustains quality partnerships. The keys to building relationships within partnerships with parents are the same as building relationships in the classroom. We need to feel like we belong, we need to be able to trust the 'other' and we need to believe that we are valued, that we matter. Relationships nurture the collaboration that is so necessary for partnerships to survive and to help individuals succeed.

We believe that settings need to ensure they have put in place the building blocks around working with parents as partners in order to give the individual with special needs the best chance of success. In acknowledging this, how do we engage more effectively with parents, and are we doing as much as we could or should?

The following is a list of questions which may prove useful for SFSE leaders to use in exploring what they are currently doing, how effective current practice is, and to examine possible additional ways to engage with parents as partners in the future.

Key Questions
1. Have you asked parents what they expect from the school?

Commonly used questionnaires often collect information on what parents think of a school, but the focus of this is much more open and is asking what parents expect. This will provide very different answers. The focus would be on what's already working and what would make it even better.

2. What do you expect from parents?

In any partnership there needs to be a two-way process of agreeing each other's roles. If this is in place, how is this worded and how was it developed? These are issues that need to be carefully thought about.

3. Have you asked parents what they think of the school?

As already raised in Question 1, this is often what parental surveys cover, but, as with all questionnaires, the key element of the usefulness of these is the quality of the questions. We would advise being very explicit in asking them about what it is you want to know. For example, in addressing their thoughts and feelings about induction:

- How welcome are they made to feel?

- How responsive is the school?

- How well has their child settled in?

4. How do you involve parents?

Is the school doing as much as it could to involve parents in the life of the school?

5. Why do some parents not get involved?

For those of us who work in the special needs field, this is a crucial area to explore. For those parents who are engaged with the school, any difficulties or concerns can generally be discussed and solutions found. What is much more of a problem is what to do when parents are not involved. Why are they not involved? The reasons, and hence some of the difficulty, can be diverse and complex, but that does not mean we should not try and remedy the situation. It must be recognised that for many parents, their experiences with school were unpleasant and may well bring back negative memories. Another factor could be language and/ or cultural barriers, or indeed the parents may also have special needs.

6. What can you do to establish an effective working relationship with the 'missing' parents?

Given that experience of their time at school can be a cause of the ineffective relationship, we believe the onus is on leaders to help break down those barriers and to engage with these 'missing' parents. In recognising this, we would also suggest that we are not always the best person to do this, as the negative parental experiences may well have been with the leader and possibly an individual teacher. Therefore, getting other professionals, or probably even better, getting *other parents*, to make the links may well be a more effective way of engaging with 'missing' parents. We also need to explore what explicit and implicit cultural messages are given out by the setting and whether these are creating a barrier. Also, do we need to make our communications with parents more than just written? Do we always expect parents to come to us?

7. What can you do to help parents to help their child?

Schools often have clear expectations of what help they expect parents to give their child, but how achievable are these? For parents of primary-aged children there is, quite rightly, an expectation of significant time spent reading with and listening to the child read. Whilst some schools are very good at supporting parents to achieve this, others just expect the parents to know *how to* support reading. For anyone involved with developing reading skills, we have all experienced how difficult this is for some children, and *we* have the training and knowledge to support them!

8. What priority do staff give to working with parents?

Without a doubt, the majority of staff in schools work extremely hard and are relatively time-poor. Some staff are excellent at making good relationships with parents, whilst for others it can be seen as an onerous activity. As leaders, we always felt that the priorities we set within the school largely set the priorities for other staff. So, as a leader, it is worth examining how much emphasis you give to working with parents, and how this manifests in practice.

- Do you regularly talk about the importance of this with staff?

- Are there skills and protocols in place for staff to establish these connections?

- Is a parent handbook in place that supports the building of a partnership, rather than one that just tells parents what happens?

- Do you actively engage with parents in public places at the beginning or end of the school day when they are dropping their children off or picking them up?

As is generally the case, to make initiatives such as partnerships with parents work, there is a commitment of time and resources needed. It is the leader who generally emphasises the importance, or not, of these initiatives. We would argue that most leaders know that a partnership with parents is important. We may have believed that we were doing all that we could, and it was up to the parents to do more. As a way forward, undertaking a review of current practice, using the questions above as a framework, could prove beneficial for all involved, particularly the children and young people with special needs. All involved in education know that we have a better chance of success if parents and the school are working together rather than against each other. This is supported by the research, which found that education is most effective when:

- families are seen as partners in the development of their child's plan

- comprehensive wraparound programmes are developed for students and families in need of intensive support

- local family support groups are fully involved in school and district development, implementation and evaluation of programmes (Cheney and Osher, 1997; Epstein, Kutash and Duchnowski, 1998).

The challenge is for each school to develop their approach to engage meaningfully with parents as partners. We shall now explore in more detail possible additional challenges when working with parents of individuals with special needs.

Highly effective settings know that there is even more importance in engaging with the parents of individuals with special needs due to the often complex nature of their needs. The families have had years of experience in knowing what the best strategies and approaches are in supporting their child. These families may have dealt with difficult situations for a number of years, yet one or more parents have continued to stay involved with his or her child. Respect for these parents is a precipitator for their engagement with the setting. Without them, useful information about how to work with their children will be lost (Brubaker, Brubaker and Link, 2001).

In relation to those individuals who display challenging behaviour, caring for such individuals can put families under great pressure, and often restricts what they are able to do. As a consequence of this, families of individuals with challenging behaviour often have emotional and physical health problems of their own. These difficulties are often made worse by the problems many families experience in getting effective help and support. Therefore, support from settings needs to be flexible and personalised to the needs and circumstances of the individual families (SCIE, 2011).

Additionally, given that many families may have experienced many years of focus on their child's difficulties, in order to get the support they need and deserve, it is important that settings have an explicit focus on the individual's strengths. Acknowledging and celebrating when things are going well, as opposed to just when there is a problem, is important in building a successful partnership with parents of individuals with special needs. All people, adults and children need to hear positive news to balance the negative, which sometimes can weigh us down when it's constant.

The challenge is for each setting to develop their approach to meaningfully engage with parents as partners. We will now go on to explore an example where this was done in a SF way.

FKC Mellansjo special school near Stockholm, Sweden

Kerstin Mahlberg and Maud Sjoblom share some interesting approaches to working with parents in their book, *Solution Focused Education* (2004). It is based on the premise that all parents want the best for their children. With this premise, it becomes easier to create good relationships with parents. The authors come from the standpoint that there is a positive intention behind everything that a person does. In their SF work, they employ a conversation methodology (creative questions) to underscore the resources, competence and abilities of pupils and parent alike, and emphasise these attributes in a way that makes them clear to the person in question. This all helps build the relationship between school and family and is more likely to lead to a more effective partnership. They also identify that they use 'reframing' with parents. When a parent describes their child in negative terms, they attempt to find a more positive word that they can weave into any new question or response they give.

The purpose in reframing is so that the parent does not feel ashamed or guilty about the negative situations that occur. Reframing is meant to evoke good feelings. This in turn facilitates co-operation between all parties and makes it easier to find shared ways to bring about an effective outcome.

At Mellansjo they very much view parents as a resource, but this is a joint responsibility. Parents are expected in school with their children for the first ten days, and after that they spend one day or half a day a week in school, for as long as their child is enrolled.

All teachers know how to manage their contacts with parents and how to deal with possible conflict. They have a stated belief that no parent should ever have to leave a meeting feeling offended or upset, stating that there is a shared responsibility for making parents feel comfortable, whether in formal meetings or informal conversation.

Whilst the expectation in relation to parents attending the school with their child both initially and longer term would not be achievable in most cases in my experience, the clear and firm commitment to seeing parents and partners as resources has much to offer in terms of providing SFSE with parents.

Person-centred education

We will now go on to explore the excellent work of Helen Sanderson Associates in their work with others in personalising education in the UK, and also in Australia and Canada.[1]

As stated in the Introduction, we are viewing the examples shared through a parent and community lens. We will draw on a few of the person-centred tools to explore further and suggest how they might be made even more SF.

Person-centred thinking tools and practices have their foundation in person-centred planning, an approach to social justice and inclusion originally developed to support people with learning disabilities. The Learning Community for Person-Centred Practices[2] developed the person-centred thinking tools and they are now evidenced-based practice, used in health and social care.

Person-centred thinking tools are essentially methodical ways to ensure that education is meeting the needs of each child or young person, recognising that each has a unique style of learning, communicating, building relationships and making decisions.

For the purposes of this chapter, we will explore possible family and community benefits from working in this way, and also suggest amendments to five of the tools and activities which could make them more SF in nature.

---

1   We would recommend viewing the information at www.personalisingeducation. org for a complete picture of what is being suggested and used.

2   See www.learningcommunity.us.

It is interesting to note that whilst the focus of the work is on person-centred practices in school, there is a clear emphasis that one of the ways of achieving this is to engage more with the family, and to a lesser extent the community.

Benefits for parents

In heading this section up as 'Benefits for parents', we consider that this implicitly means benefits for students. The starting point of each tool and activity is reviewed in relation to benefits for students. This is also explored in Chapter 5.

The main benefits identified throughout the different activities and tools are:

- the relationship between school, parents and community and what each brings that the other can value

- having the opportunity to contribute

- school having a full understanding of their child

- future focused.

In terms of valuing, a range of the tools help all involved with the student focus on the strengths and capabilities of the student. This is obviously encouraging for a parent to hear and so builds stronger relationships. The relationship circle, decision-making and roles and responsibilities tools also give an opportunity for all involved with the student a chance to value the input they are having in supporting the student.

All of the tools have a focus on involving students and parents in completing them. This opportunity to contribute in a valued way is very empowering for the family and other support people. It acknowledges the parents as experts in their child's life. It enables them to feel listened to as well as clarifying roles and responsibilities for all involved. The person-centred review enables the parents to be seen as contributing on equal terms, as opposed to just coming in to hear what the professionals think.

Involving parents in completing many of the tools encourages trust from the parents that the school has a full understanding of their child. Where the parents have a fuller understanding of the school, and the school has as much information as possible regarding communication and other key elements in supporting the student, the partnership is likely to be successful. Additionally, whilst celebrating successes and strengths, there is also a clear focus on the future and what the next steps are.

Community (others)

A number of the tools help in ensuring that key information is shared, in a positive and accessible way, with peers and the wider community the student may come into contact with. The relationship circle activity can help clarify for the parents who their child's friendship group is and can also be used to explore possible and current community opportunities. The Community Contributions tool (which explores the contributions the wider community offers to the situation) is particularly focused on exploring this side of things for the student with input from all relevant people.

Partnerships with the community: Autism at Kingwood Current Action Research Projects in collaboration with the Helen Hamlyn Centre for Design at the Royal College of Art

The following section will explore a number of examples from Autism at Kingwood,[3] a UK charity dedicated to pioneering best practices to help people with ASD and Asperger's syndrome live full and active lives. We will then also share an example of a community business case study where there was the use of a SF business planning tool. We recognise that these examples will not be relevant to all individuals with special needs, but they will be to some and there may well be ideas that emerge for other community-based partnerships.

This quote from the Autism at Kingswood website sums up their philosophy:

> Everything we do is about giving people that Kingwood supports opportunities to express themselves, to develop their interests, and to challenge themselves in a controlled way. That changes everything.

---

3   See www.kingwood.org.uk.

Despite the challenge of developing a deep understanding of people who often have limited speech and additional learning disabilities, Kingwood has invited these autistic people, their support staff, and their families into the design process as active participants.

They identify that action research plays a major role in the work undertaken at Kingwood as it strives to gain a deeper understanding of ASD and the impact this has on the lives of individuals concerned, particularly with regard to sense and perception. This new understanding is then used to inform how they deliver their services. Whilst not explicitly adopting a SF approach, we believe that their design-centred approach has many similarities and much to offer for consideration by others.

What follows is a summary of the approach and projects. For a more detailed understanding of the projects and design methodology, please see Gaudion (2015).

Approach

When designing for people with ASD, Kingwood identify that it is essential to have an understanding of how they might experience the environment and perceive people and objects in it.

In order to achieve this, the following approach was implemented. First, interviews were conducted with adults with ASD, as well as professionals who work with them such as support workers, psychologists and architects. Second, an expert reference group was established. The third element of the research study included visits to supported living residences. The purpose of conducting studies *in situ* was to observe first hand how residents use and respond to their living environments, see how support workers interact with them and carry out contextual interviews. These individuals have difficulties with communication and various stimulation sensitivities, but also a desire for independence.

Insights were drawn from the stories and observations to develop universal themes and a design guide. Throughout the project, contributors were invited to comment on the work. To get feedback on specific issues, illustrated concepts were reviewed in workshops with autistic adults.

From this work they identified four design themes summarised as follows:

1. **Growth and development**: enhance the motivation, confidence and self-esteem of residents by encouraging exploration of their environment and providing spaces for developing interests and skills.

2. **Triggers**: reduce the triggers of agitation and anxiety, by providing comprehensible, coherent spaces that meet the sensory needs of individuals.

3. **Robustness**: keep residents and staff safe in a robust environment that is tolerant of unintended use.

4. **Support tools**: give staff the tools to deliver people-centred care and support.

The Kingwood research identified that this approach to design had the following positive impacts:

Enhancing the following qualities through design can enhance health, wellbeing and quality of life
Independence

- Giving residents choice in how they live and who they share their home with is empowering.

- Enabling residents to do things by themselves increases self-esteem.

Social interaction

- Providing a variety of spaces allows residents to engage in social activities on their own terms.

- Enabling residents to adjust their home environments to the desired level of social engagement or privacy can result in increased levels of social interaction.

Access

- Allowing access to the whole building, especially outdoor spaces, creates a sense of ownership and freedom.

- Offering good access to the local neighbourhood can provide residents with purposeful activity.

Affordability

- Offering a variety of affordable housing options with graduated levels of support can help residents progress from needing significant support to living semi-independently.

Evolution

- Providing home environments that respond to the changing interests and aspirations of residents can further their self-development.

- Using features that can be deactivated or removed makes it easier to disable stimulation which may lead to focused interests and inhibit progress.

Enhancing the following qualities through design can reduce triggers that cause agitation
Sensation

- Designing consistent, low-arousal environments with appropriate lighting, acoustics, ventilation and use of colour and material can minimise sensory overload.

- Providing stimulation for residents with underdeveloped sensory sensitivities can reduce complex behaviour. In particular, environments may need to accommodate vestibular and proprioceptive activities.[4]

---

4   These refer to the vestibular system, which is a contributor to your balance system and your sense of spatial orientation, and the proprioceptive system which provides information to your brain about your body's position in relation to your environment (which direction you are facing, for example, or how close you are to obstacles).

Perception

- Designing navigable environments can help residents orientate themselves both physically and socially.

- Providing clear sensory cues as to the function of specific spaces can help residents understand what is expected of them.

- Designing permeable interiors that increase predictability and legibility can help residents assess potential social interactions.

Refuge

- Offering private spaces that can be personalised by residents, as well as withdrawal spaces peripheral to communal areas, allows residents to retreat from group situations when overwhelmed.

Empowerment

- Designing environments in which stimulation can be calibrated by residents provides a sense of control and empowerment.

Enhancing the following qualities through design can reduce risks and lessen the impact of heavy or unintended use

Safety

- Controlling access to areas of risk and using safety materials and technologies can protect residents and staff from injury.

Durability

- Using durable materials can reduce the impact of heavy or self-injurious behaviour such as jumping, banging, running and fiddling.

Ease of maintenance

- Designing environments so they can be easily maintained helps staff to spend more time supporting residents.

- If home environments are easy to maintain, residents are more likely to get involved with household tasks such as cleaning.

Tolerance

- Designing environments that can withstand unintended use can lessen the physical and emotional impact for residents when they make mistakes.

Enhancing the following qualities through design can increase levels of purposeful communication and reduce frustration

Communication

- Using visual prompts to impart information, give warnings and reinforce orientation within home environments can help residents understand what is expected of them.

- Providing tools for spontaneous non-verbal communication between residents and between residents and staff can increase interaction and enhance confidence.

- Embedding information in the environment about how it should be used can motivate residents to take on household tasks.

Personal support

- Providing appropriate environments for one-to-one life-skill training and assisting with personal hygiene care can help staff deliver quality support.

- Providing facilities for staff to record observations and capture what residents like, enjoy and respond to can improve continuity of support.

Unobtrusive monitoring

- Embedding strategies and assistive technologies in the home environment allows staff to safely monitor residents from a distance.

What now follows are specific examples where Kingwood have adopted the above design-centred approach. We would encourage you to visit their website and access the publications which share much more detail on their excellent approaches.[5]

Project 1: Autism and Housing Design

Since 2009 Kingwood has worked with the Helen Hamlyn Centre at the Royal College of Art to explore the way in which housing is designed and how this impacts on the lives of people with ASD and Asperger's. They have been focusing on how people with ASD interact with an environment that has been specifically adapted and furnished to take account of their individual sensory issues. They then went on to assess whether these adaptations minimised stress and anxiety triggers for each of the individuals involved in the project and, moreover, whether through appropriately structured stimulation within these new environments, opportunities can be developed for each person to develop new skills.

Project 2: Autism and Sensory Preference

Exploring Sensory Preferences: Living Environments for Adults with Autism (Brand and Gaudion, 2012) is the second publication in the series following Housing Design for Adults with Autism produced by Kingwood and the Helen Hamlyn Centre.

The publication describes a design research project aimed at developing ways to help adults with ASD to better manage relationships with their home environments and other people by creating living accommodation that is more sensitive to their sensory needs.

The publication draws findings from the published guide into making sensory props (*Ready Steady Make*, Gaudion, 2012) and the associated staff development workshops for support workers which promote the development of skills in understanding sensory challenges and making sensory props.

Project 3: Green Spaces

A well-designed garden can enhance focus and attention, and reduce anxiety, thereby improving quality of life. Green Spaces explores outdoor environments for adults with ASD.

---

5   www.kingwood.org.uk/kingwood-research-projects.

The publication describes how design can create useful green spaces benefitting those who use them. The researchers involved visited and consulted with specialists in sensory gardens and therapeutic gardens, in horticulture and occupational therapy. Additionally, they spent time with the people Kingwood supports and their families.

The findings presented in this publication draw upon the previous research into the built environments and practical experience to expand upon ways in which outdoor design can improve the lives of the people they support.

Project 4: Designing Everyday Activities

This is the fourth in a series that describes design research projects carried out by the Helen Hamlyn Centre for Design at the Royal College of Art in partnership with the Kingwood Trust. The overall aim of the work is to improve the everyday experiences of those with ASD through a better understanding of their needs, aspirations and physical environment.

The research investigates how those whom Kingwood support perceive everyday activities and engage with them. The project seeks to help Kingwood's support staff to develop a design framework that will help to transform or adapt everyday activities in the home. The objective is to make the ordinary extraordinary, to design activities that foster opportunities to develop skills and encourage meaningful interactions between people with ASD and Kingwood support staff. Everyday activities such as doing laundry, cleaning, cooking a meal or operating electrical appliances help us to develop life skills, to live independently and to keep our homes clean and enjoyable to live in. Most of us take this for granted even though performing these activities demands a substantial amount of body co-ordination, motivation and adaptive skills such as physical dexterity, motor skills, planning, organisational abilities and social communication skills.

As stated in the introduction to the section on Kingwood they would, quite rightly, describe their approach as design-centred, and whilst not the same as SF, we do believe there are enough common threads to warrant its inclusion in this chapter.

Edgeware Creative Entrepreneurship and Tim: making money and making meaning

We will now move to an example of a partnership between a company and an individual with disabilities and how this partnership helped lead to a meaningful and purposeful life beyond schooling.

Edgeware Creative Entrepreneurship is a training and coaching company that serves startups and early-stage businesses. Emerging from a background in community cultural development, it brings focus to the entrepreneur at the heart of every new enterprise, a person with operational *competencies* and skills, and also higher order *capabilities* like creativity, resilience and commitment. It is founded on the assumption that creative entrepreneurs set out not only to make money, but to make meaning.

Tim is such an entrepreneur. He lives in regional Queensland with a variety of disabilities and requires a high degree of care and support, with which he is fortunately blessed through a dedicated set of family and carers.

Tim completed Edgeware's 'Build Your Business' course in 2011, completing their 'one page business plan'[6] and setting it to work in his enterprise, Tim's Bloomin' Healthy Seedlings, which provides certified organic vegetable seedlings for sale at country markets. He knows that he will never make a living entirely from his business, such is the diversity of his needs, but that's not the point. The money he makes is *his*, and signals independence and choice which otherwise would be difficult to achieve.

Tim has just bought his first van, which fits his seedling stock in the back, and him, and his wheelchair.

Tim's success has been supported by many people and many factors. As far as his Edgeware experience goes, he took benefit from the trainers' radically constructivist pedagogy, what Edgeware calls 'curriculum on the fly'. The 'one page business plan' is comprised of information from a suite of simple decision-making tools, founded on the training team's experience of the basics of business, and their response to the particular context of the trainee. This is quite distinct from a set idea of 'what the training should achieve'. Education is seen as responsive, as a *leading out*.

---

6   See www.edgeware.com.au.

Strengths and resources

Tim's story shows the efficacy of a learner-centred and strengths-focused approach. As part of his one page business planning, he first details his 'NOW', his situation and context, his resources and aspirations, using a related set of simple (which is not necessarily to say 'easy') decision-making tools. These focus on the concept of value: what value does Tim's product bring into the world, and what value does Tim's customer see in that product?

Once these are understood, Tim can conceive of a value proposition, one of the first 'NOW' tools, the basis of a value exchange (a product, say, exchanged for money). The value proposition is the foundational 'NOW' statement. It tells Tim (and the market place) (1) what 'it' is; (2) who it's for; and (3) what 'who it's for' actually sees in 'what it is'.

Other 'NOW' tools identify key customer segments and key qualities of product offerings, then interrogate (in true SF style) the ideal matching of ideal customer with ideal product. This makes, in the Edgeware framework, for customer 'success'.

From this foundation, stated in brief summaries of the tool outputs, Tim ideates and details a 'WHERE', using a set of tools, once more, to help him imagine and describe a state of affairs where *everything has gone right*, where everything good that could possibly happen, has happened. He then characterises the key elements of this desired state in as much finely grained detail as possible, from the material level ('how much money am I turning over in a month?) to the very personal ('how do I feel about my relationships in this "perfect future"?'). The 'WHERE' state is not about goal-setting, but rather an ideation, SF-style, of a desired state of affairs to which to aspire, akin to business guru Steven Covey's imprecations to 'start with the end in view'.

Edgeware's 'HOW' tools, then, enable small, achievable and measurable actions which will move his business towards that ideal state, steps which link his NOW to his WHERE. For example, brainstormed ideas for action are rated for 'impact' (that is, degree of benefit for his business) and 'ease' (which is to say, ease of execution, measured in fewest resources, least effort, least expenditure). These two values are then cross-compared, enabling Tim to identify those actions which have, relative to the others, both the highest degree of impact and the highest degree of ease: the easiest ways to create greatest bang for the buck. In doing so he identifies, for practical purposes (and to take a leaf from

Pareto[7]) the 20 per cent of effort he needs to expand in order to achieve 80 per cent of the benefit.

Overall, the NOW–WHERE–HOW logic translates a realistic situation analysis into a set of discrete and achievable actions by ideating a SF future, and then methodically generating a set of actions which move the proprietor in the direction of that ideated future. Edgeware calls these TATTS – Tiny, Achievable, Tick-able Tasks.

In the process Tim used, and uses, a close and dedicated professional and family network, and the wider network engaged by them (for example, the organic growers' formal and informal networks). He used, and uses, a social-cultural shift towards the recognition, tolerance and support of people with disabilities. He used, and uses, the growing popularity of farmers' markets. And he draws on his own, on-board and inner resources, to create and practise an enterprise which engages him as a creator and provider of *value*.

Partnerships with the other services

We have so far explored the partnership with parents, partnership with a provider of adult services, and the partnership with a coaching and training company and examples of these being done well. We will now move on to explore an example of a support association which has found significant benefits from adopting a SF approach in its work.

As stated in the introduction, not all individuals with special needs are going to be accessing additional community support services, particularly the examples which are in the area of child protection and safety. However, in our experiences, some individuals will unfortunately be accessing these services and many others will access other support services who may wish to explore their provision alongside these approaches.

We are now going to share the SF approaches of a support organisation, the National Society for the Prevention of Cruelty to Children (NSPCC).

---

7   See https://en.wikipedia.org/wiki/Pareto_principle.

NSPCC's Face to Face Service SF Toolkit (2014)
Background

The NSPCC's Face to Face service has been delivered in 18 locations in the UK. The service is offered to children and young people in care and those on the edge of care who wish to receive support and can identify something that they wish to change in their life. Trained NSPCC practitioners work with the children and young people using a solution focused approach, to identify how the child can make positive changes in their life to achieve their wishes. Practitioners delivering the Face to Face service received introductory training in using solution focused practice.

The NSPCC has been using solution focused practice with children and young people in their Face to Face service since September 2011. Through this work our practitioners have developed a wealth of knowledge in communicating different aspects of the solution focused approach to children of varying ages, interests and needs.

The toolkit was first developed by NSPCC practitioners to support themselves and their colleagues in conducting solution focused work with children and young people aged five to 19. The toolkit has been developed to help people who have already received training in using a solution focused approach with children and young people. It provides practical materials and resources that can be used specifically with children and young people.

We would highly recommend accessing the toolkit as there are a wide range of tools that could be of use in a wide range of circumstances. What follows now are some key principles found by the NSPCC in adopting and using the toolkit.

Problem-free talk

The toolkit identifies that when the practitioner first meets the child or young person, it will be important to learn some things from them: their interests, skills and strengths. This information will help you to plan future sessions and select suitable tools and activities that fit the child's interests.

They also note that where they refer to 'problem-free talk' this is not just limited to verbal discussion, it could be other forms of interaction like drawing, play-acting or other activities.

Engaging in problem-free talk provides a positive start to the solution focused process. Inviting the child to describe their likes and strengths will communicate to them that there is more to them than just the problem. This way you and the child will be reminded of the resourceful person who has abilities and skills. At this point you have the opportunity to re-frame the child's thinking around their strengths, so that they can start to see themselves in a different, more positive way. Building these positive references supports the child to begin considering other possibilities and to become hopeful that change is possible. As a practitioner you can also use problem-free talk to show that you are choosing to work with a resourceful and capable child who has lots of positive qualities, rather than perceiving the child as difficult and troublesome.

With younger children it may take some time to help them identify their hopes for this work. Playing a game or carrying out a 'getting to know you' activity may help you to learn what is important to them. These activities may also help you to find out about their 'solution team' – this is the people in their life who can offer them support and encouragement.

Things to consider
Bear in mind that it is the aim of problem-free talk to help the child to discover positive things about themselves. However, if a child needs to unburden themselves, they may need to spend some time talking about problems at the outset of a session, to get this off their chest. Your role as a practitioner will be to listen to them and acknowledge what they tell you, while listening out for ways that you can draw the conversation towards solutions. For example, you may say 'That sounds difficult, how did you cope with that situation?'

Other things to consider at the outset of the work include:

- What does the child or young person like?

- Are they particularly active, creative or imaginative?

- Do they enjoy role playing, drawing or listening to and telling stories?

- If the child is shy, would it be helpful to have some activities that do not require a lot of direct eye contact?

- It may be useful to draw on third-party reports, by saying 'What would a friend say about you?'

Establishing what is wanted: the destination of the work

The process of establishing what the child or young person wants from your work with them is also known as finding out their 'best hopes' or establishing a contract with them (Shennan, 2014). This is an essential part of the process as the child or young person's best hopes will become the focus for your subsequent work with them.

There may be times when other agencies, carers or family members will make suggestions in relation to the focus of the work. Although this can be considered, the contracting must be with the child or young person. Therefore, it is the child's best hope that should be the focus throughout.

When asking children about their best hopes, NSPCC practitioners have experienced a variety of answers, ranging from a shrug of the shoulders to 'I dunno' to 'Feel better about myself' to 'Stop being so angry' to 'Wanting to move back to mum', to name but a few. The challenge is to formulate a 'best hope' that is achievable for the child, so that the work can progress toward this.

Harry Korman (2004), cited in Ratner, George and Iveson (2012), has given some clear guidance on the criteria that the child or young person's 'best hopes' need to meet as part of the solution focused process.

These are:

1. Something that the client wishes to achieve, which

2. Fits with the practitioner's legitimate remit, and which

3. The practitioner and client working well together could hope to achieve.

Some children may readily be able to identify what they want from the work, but others may need some help to identify what is important to them, and what they would like to focus on during their time with you (the solution focused practitioner).

To keep the work in a solution focused mindset, it is important that the child's best hopes are phrased in positive terms, for example 'I'd like to have more friends' rather than 'I want to feel less lonely'.

A variety of questions can be used, together with tools and resources, to ask the child or young person what they would like to achieve through your work together. These might include:

- What are your best hopes for our work together?

- Is there anything that you would like to change in your life?

- And if you changed that, what would be different about you?

- What would be different if the 'problem' was not here?

- How would you know that our time together has helped you?

Describe what is wanted in detail: the preferred future

This part of the work enables the child or young person to start describing a future in which they have moved towards achieving their best hopes. This is often referred to as the child's 'preferred future'. One of the means of helping people to describe their preferred future is through the use of the 'Miracle Question'. The origins of the Miracle Question, first developed by Insoo Kim Berg, are discussed by Guy Shennan in his book *Solution Focused Practice* (2014, pp.49–52).

Once the child has identified their best hopes for the work, you can move on to this part of the process – that is, helping the child to describe their preferred future. However, if you move on to this part of the work before a clear contract (the child's best hopes) has been identified and agreed, this could become confusing for you and the child, and could get in the way of a focused piece of work.

This step of the process is important because it helps the child or young person to envisage the future, with their best hopes achieved, and to bring this to life as a possibility. The process asks the child to describe 'how they would know/what they see/what do they do/who notices?' when their best hopes are happening and then to build detail around their description. In the details they describe, the child will find the building blocks of their solutions, which are already taking place and which they may be able to do more of. It is important to gain detail and build ideas of what else is possible.

This activity is also valuable because it will give the young person clues about the future they are seeking to move towards, how they might get there and how this may affect them and other people around them in a positive way.

The purpose of children describing their preferred future is to release their imagination of what is possible and what can be. Some children and young people will be able to describe their preferred future if they are simply invited to. You could initiate the conversation in this way: 'Suppose, when you wake up tomorrow, you find that [insert whatever their best hopes are here] is happening – what's the first thing you'd notice about yourself?'

It works well to start with the first thing the child would notice as you can then encourage them to describe their whole day from start to finish, with lots of detail: what they would be doing, how they would feel, what they would do, what they would notice, what other people would notice. Please see the tools in this section which pose a variety of questions you may wish to ask the child or young person.

Encourage the child or young person to add as much detail as possible to their description of their preferred future. Be mindful of not moving on too quickly from this stage of the process.

Things to consider

- Make sure that the way you discuss this with the child or young person is appropriate to their age, interests and cultural background.

- Note that scenarios involving miracles or magic may not be appropriate for all children.

- Might the child wish to share their best hopes and their preferred future with a member of their 'solution team'?

Working toward the preferred future: instances, exceptions and scaling questions

A great deal of solution focused work will be about working with the child or young person to identify behaviours and activities that are already helping them move towards their preferred future, and that can help them move closer still.

For example, a child may want to get on better with their foster carer. In one session, the child may identify that they get on better with their foster carer when they help out a bit more. Then between sessions they may practise times of doing this.

At the next session they may report back on how this helped, who noticed and how this left them feeling, and can consider what else they are doing that is making a difference, and what other small differences might look like.

Instances, exceptions and scaling questions are important aspects of the process for solution focused work.

Instances

An instance refers to an aspect of the preferred future that has already happened or is happening. Discussion of instances will help the child to stay close to the positive vision of their preferred future, and to consider how they are already moving towards their hopes. It is preferable to discuss the preferred future in relation to instances rather than exceptions, as exceptions are framed in relation to the problem, whereas instances are framed in relation to the solution.

If a young person's best hope was to get on better with her mum, an example of an instance might be 'This week I was able to stay downstairs and watch TV with my mum and we got on OK'.

This activity might work well alongside or following an exercise to identify the child's solution team, as the child may wish to include members of their solution team in the scene they create.

Exceptions

It can be useful to discuss exceptions in situations where a child or young person is very stuck in talking about their problems and is struggling to describe their preferred future. It might also be useful in a follow-up session if the child is finding it hard to discuss 'what is better' and is talking about problems that have occurred since the last meeting. In these circumstances, it might be helpful for them to think about exceptions to these situations, when the problem was not a problem.

This process can help the child to recognise that the problem is not a problem all the time, and to think of ways that they can build on their existing strengths and coping skills.

Following on from the previous example, an example of an exception might be 'This week I was able to stay downstairs and watch TV with my mum and we didn't have an argument that day'.

Scaling questions

Scaling questions are a means of eliciting examples of instances and exceptions. During this stage you are looking for 'news of difference' when parts of the preferred future are already happening. In doing this it is useful to introduce a scaling activity, making the top of the scale the child or young person's preferred future and the bottom of the scale as remote from the preferred future as possible. When the child or young person chooses a value on the scale to represent where they feel they are now in relation to their preferred future, the number itself is not important to the worker, although of course it is to the child. The worker is not assessing the child here, and is not evaluating the meaning of the number. The number only becomes meaningful when the detail is shared by the child or young person of what the number means for them and what it says about what is already taking place.

The key function of the scaling is that the child or young person is supported to express the finer details of where they are now and what they are already doing in relation to their preferred future. This description will undoubtedly start to introduce instances and exceptions that can be explored further and built upon.

Scaling questions are used to break down the preferred future into small actions/steps, thus asking the child or young person to describe what one step on the scale looks like and what a step up the scale would look like.

It is important not to move up the scale too quickly, and to draw out a lot of detail about what the child is doing to be at the point they have reached on the scale (this is one of the hardest aspects of practising the approach). By focusing on what the child is already doing that is working, the child will be better able to do more of this, to find other strategies and try new ideas, and sometimes even to realise that they are already further up the scale than they thought.

For example, if the child or young person is currently at number three on the scale, you might ask them 'What are you doing to be at number three rather than two or one?'

The solution team

The 'solution team' is a term for describing people in the child or young person's life who support them and will be able to help them work towards achieving their best hopes. Members of the solution team may include parents or carers, siblings and teachers at school.

Following discussion of the child's best hopes and preferred future, it may be a helpful exercise to ask who they would choose to put in their solution team. You can then discuss how the child can draw on these sources of support to help them move in the right direction.

It may be appropriate, particularly with younger children, to ask if they want to involve a parent or carer in the work. Ways that a parent/carer or other member of the child's network may be able to help include:

- being aware of the child's best hopes and encouraging the child to stick to the strategies they have identified

- noticing when the child makes progress between sessions and providing positive feedback

- in some cases, attending the first session and/or subsequent sessions to help put the child at ease and facilitate communication between the child and the worker (this may be particularly relevant with younger children or children with learning difficulties).

Building on success

It is important to note that a lot of the key work that the child or young person is doing will be taking place in between sessions. Berg and Steiner (2003) refer to 'homework' and 'experiments' as ways that the child or young person can build on their achievements and strategies in between sessions.

Ending sessions

The endings of sessions are opportunities to help a child or young person sum up what they have learned during the meeting and to consider how they might put these insights into practice during the time before your next meeting. The 'checklist' activity[8] may be one way to help the child get involved with this summing-up process, and to give them a reminder of what they can focus on in the coming days.

---

8   See https://learning.nspcc.org.uk/research-resources/2015/solution-focused-practice-toolkit.

It is also valuable to offer the child appreciation for the efforts they have made during the session and the ideas and strategies they have identified.

At the end of the session, it may be helpful to discuss what the child will try to practise or 'notice' before the next session. You may want to discuss a way that they can record times when this happens as 'moments of success' in between sessions. This may be something that a member of their solution team could be involved with (for example, noticing when the child is exhibiting positive behaviours that they are working on and making a note of this).

Follow-up sessions

Follow-up sessions should start with asking the child or young person to reflect on what has changed for the better since the last meeting. What strategies that they have used worked well?

To help personalise the experience for the child and make this feel like a cohesive piece of work, it can be helpful to use the child's own language and 'in-jokes' to show them that you have remembered what they told you last time. It is often useful to bring the child's work from previous sessions with you, so that you can refer back to it and build on previous conversations.

Planning and working toward endings

Solution focused practice is designed to support short-term interventions that empower children and young people. When offering a stand-alone intervention, the solution focused practitioner is there to help the child or young person in the context of their existing support network (for example, parents, foster carers, teachers or other professionals), but not to replace these important adults.

Within this intervention it remains important for the practitioner to develop a good working relationship with the child or young person within the context of solution focused practice. Therefore, the practitioner will need to be clear about their particular role in the child's life and the number of sessions available to the child, so that the child is aware that they can choose to end the work when they wish, and is prepared for when the allocated sessions will come to an end.

Practitioners working on the NSPCC's Face to Face service have developed a variety of ideas for introducing this concept into sessions and providing children and young people with reminders of their achievements during the solution focused work, which they can take away with them.

This section on planning endings may be less relevant to you if you are providing solution focused support to a child or young person whom you will have an ongoing relationship with (for example, if you are a foster carer or social worker). However, with any solution focused work it could be useful for the child or young person to have a record of their strengths, coping skills and achievements they have made, which they can keep after the work has ended.

Conclusion

We believe this chapter has necessarily covered a wide and diverse number of examples. Greater involvement of the family, community and supporting services, as appropriate, are key elements to adopting a more solutions focused approach to special education. We also believe that they are key partners both whilst the student is in school and also in providing appropriate opportunities post school as the case studies demonstrate.

We hope that we have given an insight, albeit briefly, on both the importance of and possible approaches to building more effective collaboration between:

- student

- family

- school

- other professionals

- community

with the focus being on establishing and sustaining a future-focused relationship, exploring ways of extending engagement for the student both whilst they are in school and into adulthood.

References

Berg, I.K. and Steiner, T. (2003) *Children's Solution Work*. London: W.W. Norton & Company.

Brand, A. and Gaudion, K. (2012) *Exploring Sensory Preferences: Living Environments for Adults with Autism*. London: Helen Hamlyn Centre for Design.

Brubaker, T.H., Brubaker, E. and Link, M. (2001) 'School violence: partnerships with families for school reform.' *Michigan Family Review,* 6(1), 1–11.

Cheney, D. and Osher, T. (1997) 'Collaborate with families.' *Journal of Emotional and Behavioral Disorders*, 5(1), 36–40.

Epstein, M.H., Kutash, K. and Duchnowski, A.J. (eds) (1998) *Outcomes for Children with Emotional and Behavioral Disorders and Their Families: Program and Evaluation Best Practices* (Second edition). Austin, TX: Pro-Ed.

Furman, B. (2006) *Kids' Skills: Playful and Practical Solution-Finding with Children*. St Luke's Innovative Resources.

Gaudion, K. (2012) *Ready, Steady, Make: A Guide to Making Sensory Props*. Available at www.researchgate.net/publication/256547393_A_guide_to_making_sensory_props.

Gaudion, K. (2015) *A Designer's Approach: Exploring how Autistic Adults with Additional Learning Disabilities Experience their Home Environment*. PhD thesis, Royal College of Art.

Mahlberg, K. and Sjoblom, M. (2004) *Solution Focused Education*. Stockholm: Mareld.

Ratner, H., George, E. and Iveson, C. (2012) *Solution Focused Brief Therapy: 100 Key Points and Techniques*. Hove: Routledge.

SCIE (2011) 'Challenging behaviour: a guide for family carers on getting the right support for children.' In S.C.I.f. Excellence (ed.) At a glance information sheet 34: SCIE.

Shennan, G. (2014) *Solution Focused Practice: Effective Communication to Facilitate Change*. Basingstoke: Palgrave Macmillan.

Williams, P. (2015) 'How do we build effective parent–school relationships in inclusive schools?' Available at https://inclusiveschools.org/how-do-we-build-effective-parent-school-partnerships-in-inclusive-schools/ (accessed 2/10/2018).

Wolfendale, S. (ed.) (1997) *Partnership with Parents in Action*. NASEN.

Chapter 8

CONCLUSION

Nick Burnett

Critical realism, Solutions Focused Special Education and Futures Thinking

Drawing the above three 'ways of thinking' together may help to make sense of where to go from here. SF is inherently futures focused and, I believe, sits well with the field of Futures Thinking which I'll explore in a bit more detail shortly.

As identified in the Introduction, the philosophical stance that I bring to my writing is critical realism which has a number of key tenets described in that chapter. I want to draw particular attention to a few of these that are most relevant to this chapter and why I'm using Futures Thinking to help identify where to go from here.

- *All knowledge is fallible and transient.* In the critical realism literature these are seen as two separate tenets but I've joined them as they seem to be a crucial underlying viewpoint to adopt if we are to move in a different direction and not get locked in to proving one viewpoint is right and another wrong. This is particularly relevant to two of the 'elephants' identified in the Introduction: disability as an unnecessary duality, and special education versus inclusion. My view is that if we are focused on what we want rather than on defending positions we are more likely to move in a useful direction. Saying this and doing this are very different challenges but using the 'Futures Cone' explored later is a way of opening up forward-facing discussions.

- *Human action has transformational potential.* This is also linked to another key tenet of critical realism: *individuals both reproduce and transform social structures.* If we keep doing what we've always been doing, we'll keep getting what we've always got. Much of education as a whole has, in my view, been about tinkering at the edges as opposed to a fundamental exploration of what might and should be. This is another reason to adopt Futures Thinking and strategies to explore what transformations we wish to bring about.

In many ways the genesis for the idea of Solutions Focused Special Education (SFSE) began with thinking about a 'Future Perfect' for special education, which, if implemented successfully, might actually mean there is no 'special' provision needed within education. In attempting to stay true to the solutions aspect of SFSE, as opposed to finding *the* solution, I believe Futures Thinking both sits well as a SF approach and provides a range of lenses to explore what might be. In doing so it might be more accurate to rename Future Perfect and Future Perfects in this example.

Futures Thinking

I will start with a brief introduction to the field of 'Futures Thinking' before using the Futures Cone to both examine what has emerged from the chapters so far and also to explore possible SFSE futures. This section is intended to some extent to be provocative in nature to stimulate further discussion and debate with the hope of avoiding the dualities identified in the Introduction – the first two 'elephants'.

Many in this field deliberately prefer the term 'futures' as opposed to 'future'. This sits very well with my opening discussion around 'solutions' as opposed to 'solution'. Futurists use the plural of 'futures' because the master concept of the futures field is that of the existence of many potential *alternative futures*, rather than simply a single future (Voros, 2001).

Futurists' work is based on the following premises:

- *The future is not predetermined.* At the most fundamental level of nature, the physical processes of the universe are inherently indeterminate. Given this, how could any future stemming out of present physical processes be anything other than indeterminate also? Therefore, there is no, and cannot be, any *single* predetermined future; rather there are considered to be infinitely many potential *alternative* futures.

- *The future is not predictable.* Although this sounds similar to the previous premise, it is quite different, for the following reason. *Even if the future were predetermined*, we could never collect enough information about it to an arbitrary degree of accuracy to construct a complete model of how it would develop. And because the future is *not* predetermined, predictability is *doubly* impossible; we are therefore able, and forced, to make *choices* among the many potential alternative futures.

- *Future outcomes can be influenced by our choices in the present.* Even though we can't determine which future of an infinite possible variety will eventuate, nevertheless we can influence the shape of the future which does eventuate by the choices we make regarding our actions (or inaction) in the present (*in*action is also a choice). These choices have *consequences* and so they need to be made as wisely as we know how.

(Voros, 2001)

Joseph Voros (2015), an eminent Futurist, has developed and refined a model to be used to explore the types of six potential futures as shown in Figure 8.1.

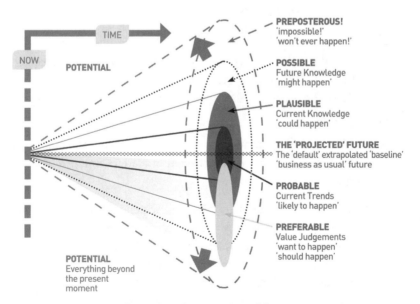

Figure 8.1: The six potential futures
Source: Adapted and extended from Voros (2003)

The idea of the Futures Cone as shown in Figure 8.1 is to identify a range of possible futures or 'lenses'. I will now share a brief explanation of the 'lens' alongside my thoughts on what the potential futures might look like as a framework to review what this might mean for SF(S)E. I've deliberately added the parenthesis to 'Special' as in a number of these, there is no such 'label'. As stated earlier, some of these can be viewed as being deliberately provocative, and I make no excuse for this, and genuinely hope they are!

SFSE Futures Thinking
Potential

This is everything beyond the present moment including what we can imagine as well as what we cannot imagine, and links well with the critical realist view of knowledge as being both fallible and transient. As the foundation of Futures Thinking, the future is not pre-determined, inevitable or 'fixed', and so what follows are my brief thoughts on what viewing the future through the different future lenses might look like. This isn't intended to be 'crystal ball gazing' suggesting that any of these might come about; it is more about what might be and what we want, as in the critical realist stance, we do influence the 'future'.

Projected

This is the continuation of progression from past experiences projected into the future. A number of the case studies shared in the previous chapters identify the early emergence of what might become more widespread practice:

- Chapter 2 – the adoption of SF Leadership competencies and practices being adopted by education leaders in an increasing number of settings.

- Chapter 3 – the approach of Finland which focuses on difficulty as opposed to disability, which therefore suggests it is transient and often linked to environment and context, as opposed to permanent, therefore drawing on the premise that elements of both the medical and the social construction of disability could be of importance at any particular time.

- Chapter 4 – SF training and mentoring being used in a larger number of environments to upskill current and future leaders and practitioners in how to use and implement SF approaches in their settings, SF human resources practices being built in as opposed to bolted on.

- Chapter 5 – the increasing awareness and use of person-centred planning as an approach to really bring about individualised learning. Additionally, the greater inclusion of students and parents in the planning and delivery of personalised approaches.

- Chapter 6 – the use of SF Coaching at an individual level with students requiring additional support alongside the widespread use of WoWW as a classroom approach to supporting behaviour.

- Chapter 7 – the examples of SF approaches being used in a wider range of community and support services, both during and after the completion of compulsory schooling.

Overall, it could be summarised as there being significant potential of a shift to more SF practice within special education and education more generally, particularly at an individual school level.

Probable

Those readers who have been in education for many years will understand that change, although happening all the time, is often painfully slow in education and often using metrics and data that many would argue are not useful/helpful or where we should be focused. If education as a whole does not shift the debate and dialogue away from largely things that are just easy to measure, there is a risk that even the case studies shared cannot continue in their current form. Often settings and educators are discouraged from risk-taking and adopting different approaches, which can lead to stagnation of practice, or a one-size-fits-all approach not only across similar settings but across countries. This is counter to adopting a SF approach which encourages the creation of 'practice-based evidence' which may well be different in every setting.

Possible

It is quite possible that the stories from the case studies and other information about exponential technologies are going to have even further impact across education, enabling more individualised support and learning opportunities for all. Special education could possibly be impacted at an even greater level than mainstream education with students getting more and better support through the use of these exponential technologies. This could even reach a point where it is easier, and more appropriate, for them to be educated alongside their mainstream peers, and therefore special education would not be needed.

What follows are a couple of examples where the use of exponential technologies is already happening.

CASE STUDY 1: HAMISH ALLAN-CANEY AT ALLENVALE SCHOOL, CHRISTCHURCH, NEW ZEALAND

As many readers will fully understand, for students with sensory challenges like ASD, everyday experiences like popping down to the supermarket, crossing the road or swimming in the sea can be absolutely terrifying.

At Allenvale School, Hamish and colleagues have introduced something to try and bridge this gap. They managed to get support from electronics giant Samsung to enable them to purchase a number of Virtual Reality (VR) goggles. Virtual Reality is an immersive multimedia or computer-simulated reality.

Allenvale School have created a mobile sensory room as one example of how VR can be used to enable greater support and access for students. Hamish is keen to point out that VR is a tool not a toy, and they have started to develop a process to introduce the use of VR apps with students:

1. Start with using Augmented Reality (AR) (Augmented Reality is the putting of computer-simulated objects within the world and is often accessed directly through a mobile phone, for example Pokemon Go).

2. Introduce VR with a 'passive' immersive experience, for example 360° video.

3. Introduce apps where the students get sensory input, for example a roller coaster ride.

They also note that VR can be used for both consumption and creation of experiences that can be useful for individual students.

An example shared in the news[1] is about ten-year-old Kingston Friggin who, through accessing VR, is now enjoying school, where he once hated it. It took staff four months of hard work preparing Kingston to try the VR goggles, but now he can't get enough of them. 'I can see a brachiosaurus! It's a herbivore. We're gonna see the tyrannosaurus rex!' Kingston says with glee. His mum says it's all steps towards Kingston engaging with reality without a digital filter. 'I think it's definitely helped him come out of his shell a lot,' Lytoya says.

Allenvale School are currently collaborating with a local high school whose senior students are working on developing VR apps for the students at Allenvale.

CASE STUDY 2: **MALIBU SCHOOL, WESTERN AUSTRALIA**

Richard Charlton

Richard has fairly recently moved from teaching in mainstream education and has brought lots of highly innovative and creative ways of using technology to enable greater and more varied and exciting learning opportunities with below just a small selection of what's being offered:

1. Using VR to enable Year 4 students to experience a Space Shuttle mission.

2. Using AR cards and coding apps.

3. Using the Metaverse app to create customised AR apps for the teaching of maths.[2]

4. Use of robot Botley to introduce the idea of coding.[3]

---

1 See www.tvnz.co.nz/one-news/new-zealand/virtual-reality-technology-helping-kids-sensory-challenges-like-autism-v1.
2 See https://gometa.io.
3 See https://www.learningresources.com/text/botley/index.html.

5. Use of drones to understand the concept 'bird's eye view'.

6. Sensorium providing an interactive multi-sensory adventure co-piloting a spaceship across the galaxy.[4]

There are a range of technologies that are being called exponential, such as:

- Artificial Intelligence (AI)

- Extended Reality (XR) – such as Virtual Reality (VR) and Augmented Reality (AR)

- Robotics

- 3D and 4D Printing

- Blockchain

- Brain Computer Interfaces (BCIs)

- Quantum Computing

- Internet of Things (IoT).

I will explore Artificial Intelligence (AI) as an example of possible impacts, however all are likely to have some form of impact in the not-too-distant future.

AI technologies are well suited to achieving crucial education objectives, such as enhancing teaching efficiency and effectiveness, providing education for all, and developing the skills that will be essential in the twenty-first century.

It is highly likely to be impacting in the following areas:

- *Enhancing individualised learning* – AI has the potential to truly bring about individualised learning which has been spoken about for a number of years. This is likely to be achieved through enhancing adaptive learning, recuperating course and content structure, and providing suitable and useful feedback.

- *Augmenting the role of the teacher* – AI has the potential to transform the role of the teacher to becoming a learning facilitator, as opposed to currently spending significant time on

---

4   See http://www.sensoriumtheatre.com.au.

planning, developing and marking in relation to set content and curriculum.

- *Augmenting educational leadership* – as in many other sectors, the role of AI to enhance and augment leadership is significant, from helping with human resources type activities, to assisting in scenario and strategy planning. The role of AI in assisting educational leaders to be even more effective is significant.

However, the success of AI in education hinges not only on technical issues but also on ethical issues, starting with, for example, who owns data on students, who can see it, who can use it, and for what purposes.

It is important to note that I am not suggesting that the future is just about technologies, but these are a few examples of opportunities that are emerging that may have a significant impact in adopting a more SF approach in not only special education, but education generally.

Preferable

As discussed in the Introduction's section on special education versus inclusion, there are very few people who would argue against the moral rationale for inclusion. For many, and I would include myself in this, there has been no clear and resource-supported plan as to how to implement this effectively. I have not seen the necessary support and training to enable this not to negatively impact on the individual student. So, my preferable future is that there is a planned and adequately resourced change management strategy in place at a system level to phase out the need for special education. This would need to provide the level of support and training to enable all students to access a truly individualised co-created 'curriculum' to meet the specific needs and desires of those individuals, their families and communities. This view might well sit in the final futures lens 'Preposterous' for many, but I believe as challenging and difficult as it is, it's not unimaginable to me.

Preposterous

There are obviously many things that could be put in here including some of my earlier 'futures' for some readers. However, to push readers' thinking to its limits (there are an increasing number of people who not only believe these but are actively trying to bring them about!), I'm just going to name a few things and let them sit with the reader, and would encourage readers to 'dream' up their own:

1. Schools are all run by robots.

2. There are no schools.

3. We become an inter-planetary species and so are not on Earth.

4. We merge with AI.

5. We can edit any disabilities 'out' of the human genome so there are no individuals with a disability.

Final thoughts

I want to finish with a return to the third 'elephant': SFSE – a paradox? My hope and belief is that not only is SFSE not a paradox but it may well be a useful way to bring about practical and inclusive strategies for all educators. Furthermore, I would like to challenge you to start, or continue, creating the 'evidence-based' practice to enable more practical and inclusive strategies to be developed for all educators.

References

Voros, J. (2001) *A Primer on Futures Studies*. Available at https://static1.squarespace.com/static/580c492820099e7e75b9c3b4/t/58abbe7c29687fbaf4a03324/1487650430788/A+Primer+on+Futures+Studies.pdf (accessed 2/10/2018).

Voros, J. (2003) 'A generic foresight process framework.' *Foresight*, 5(3), 10–21. doi:10.1108/14636680310698379.

Voros, J. (2015) *On Examining Preposterous Futures*. Available at https://thevoroscope.com/2015/12/28/on-examining-preposterous-futures (accessed 2/10/2018).

The Contributors

Drew Allison is Director of Positive Creative Solutions and Principal Tutor Team-Teach Asia Pacific. He has more than 28 years' experience in teaching, principalship, training, facilitation and consultation in the UK, Australia, New Zealand, Kenya and Jamaica.

Drew has a Bachelor of Education (Hons) from the University of Gloucestershire, the National Professional Qualification for Headship, and is a Professional Member of the Institute for Learning Professionals and the Institute of Conflict Management.

Neil Birch is the executive headteacher of the Beacon in Folkestone, England. The Beacon is a special school for 350 pupils aged between four and 19 years with profound, severe and complex learning needs. Neil is a National Leader of Education and has been involved in successfully supporting school improvement in both mainstream and special schools. He leads the CLASS Teaching School Alliance on behalf of the 24 Kent special schools. Neil has led county-wide special educational needs (SEN) development. Neil is committed to solution focused working and has been published as a research associate of the National College for Teaching and Leadership for his work on Solution Focused School Leadership. He has a strong commitment to values-led school leadership which has collaboration, joint practice and school-led improvement at its heart. A champion for vulnerable young people on both the local and the national stage, Neil believes in valuing the contribution of every individual, to bring about personal, organisational and system-wide success.

Kathleen Brown, PhD is a lecturer at California State University Channel Islands and formerly a tenured associate professor at Northeastern Illinois University in Illinois. Kathleen has been involved in multiple research projects and training initiatives in the field of special education and has presented her work at several international conferences. The origins of this solution focused assessment project began while working as a Visiting Scholar for Erasmus Mundus in Europe in 2008–2009.

Nick Burnett is an Education and Learning Entrepreneur and Futurist. He is an experienced trainer, facilitator, author, presenter and coach, who has a particular interest and expertise in the areas of coaching, leadership, special education and behaviour support with a focus on the future and the present.

He has been a teacher, senior leader and school principal and, since 2004, coach, trainer and consultant primarily to those in education, but also to others in the not-for-profit sector.

Throughout his time in education, spanning over 30 years, Nick has been committed to developing individuals at all levels, including students, and has a strong belief that everyone can develop, improve and achieve. He is committed to helping individuals and organisations 'be the best they can be'.

Since 2004, Nick has run training and facilitation for well over 5000 people, presented at numerous conferences, and has written for a wide range of publications, including authoring books on leadership, behaviour support and restorative practices. Prior to this he was recognised as an 'excellent leader' of an all-age, large special school provision in the UK.

Jenny Cole trained as a special education teacher and was a principal of special schools for 12 years. In her role of President of the WA Education Support Principals Association she advocated on a state, national and international level for students with disabilities. She is now a consultant and accredited coach, supporting schools to combine psychology, educational research and leadership theory to create flourishing individuals, schools and workplaces.

Michael Doneman is founding director of Edgeware Creative Entrepreneurship. He has a background in education and community cultural development which inspired work in business design, vocational education and training, and information technology. Michael founded the Edgeware model of ethical entrepreneurship development in 2006. He has a coaching practice focused on the generic value of creativity in the growth of entrepreneurs, intrapreneurs and leaders.

Dominik Godat is co-director of the Center for Solution Focused (SF) Leadership (www.solutionfocusedleadership.com) together with Elfie Czerny. They support individuals, leaders, teams and organisations in their development and organise a yearly SF Leadership conference in the German language (www.impulskonferenz.com). He is the author of the first worldwide research on SF Leadership and the book series 'Lösungen auf der Spur – Wirkungsvoll führen dank Lösungsfokus'. For years he was in charge of the 'CAS Coaching as leadership competence' at the Business School of the University of Applied Sciences Lucerne. He has trained a couple of thousand leaders in applying SF in their leadership function. As member of SOLworld he has been part of the development of the SF approach in organisations and was initiator of SF random coaching in 2006. With his coaching cards he has influenced more than 2000 coaches worldwide. At the moment he is travelling the world with his family in their SF RV spreading their enthusiasm for the SF approach (www.sfontour.com). Their weekly SIMPLY FOCUS podcast (www.sfontour.com/simplyfocuspodcast) features SF ideas and practitioners.

Tiina Itkonen, PhD is an associate professor of education and political science at CSU Channel Islands. Her research focuses on special education policy and politics, and is widely published internationally. She holds two honorary senior permanent lecturer positions in her native Finland in Finnish and Swedish. Prior to her position in academia, she was a special education teacher, school district specialist, and a state office project coordinator.

Dr Geoffrey James is a biologist, a teacher, a Solutions Focused Brief Therapist (SFBT) and Solutions Focused Coach. He has been successfully working with children close to permanent exclusion, with mental health challenges, special educational needs and social and economic disadvantage, as well as with adults since 2001. He has used the approach in schools, Local Authority Children's Services and the Child and Adolescent Mental Health Service. His ability to use the Solutions Focused approach with fidelity has resulted in the reliable achievement of client's best hopes, often in very complex and demanding situations. As a published author and having trained many people in Solutions Focused Coaching practice, he has a well-developed understanding of this work and its potential to bring about rapid and lasting beneficial change with clients of all ages.

Professor Eileen Munro is Professor of Social Policy at the London School of Economics. Eileen was a social worker for many years and has also studied philosophy which has fuelled her interest in the reasoning skills needed in social work. Professor Munro has written extensively on how best to combine intuitive and analytic reasoning in risk assessment and decision-making in child protection; her most well-known book *Effective Child Protection* is now in its second edition. In May 2011, Professor Munro completed the Munro Review of the English Child Protection System. The Review describes the limits of a policy of bureaucratic control in the prevention of severe child abuse arguing for growing a system that values and organises around front-line professional expertise. More information about Eileen is available at www2.lse.ac.uk.

Terry Murphy is Executive Director at Resolutions Consultancy in Perth, Western Australia with primary responsibility to coordinate key international Signs of Safety system-wide implementations and to lead and advise the licensed Signs of Safety consultants. From 2007 to 2014, Terry was the Director-General of the Department of Child Protection and Family Support (DCPFS) Western Australia, which has more than 2200 employees serving the State of 2.5 million square kilometres and 2.5 million inhabitants. In early 2008, the Western Australian Government, Terry and the DCPFS Executive made the decision to implement the Signs of Safety as its framework for all child protection practice throughout the agency. From that time under Terry's leadership, and actively involving all levels of the organisation, the Signs of Safety implementation has been central in transforming the agency, its culture and practice outcomes. Terry holds degrees in psychology and economics, as well as an MBA.

Henri Pesonen, PhD is a University Lecturer of Special Education at the University of Helsinki. His research focuses on the factors associated with sense of belonging for students with diverse learning needs, and how to support belonging in many educational contexts. His related interests include educational policy implementation. Prior to earning his PhD, he was a special education teacher in Finland, and language teacher and academic coach in the US.

Lee Shilts, PhD has been practising and researching solution focused therapy for three decades. He is co-author and developer of the Working on What Works (WoWW) programme. Lee is currently a Core Faculty professor at Capella University. He is an Approved Supervisor with AAMFT as well as a licensed family therapist in the state of Florida.

Professor Andrew Turnell is Social Work Professor of Practice at Cumbia University. Andrew is the principal co-creator of the Signs of Safety approach to child protection casework which is the most well-known participatory approach currently available in the international child protection field. Andrew leads a 60-strong international community of licensed Signs of Safety trainers and consultants hailing from Japan, New Zealand, Europe and North America. Andrew is also partner with Professor Eileen Munro and Terry Murphy in Munro, Turnell and Murphy Consulting, which works with governments and children's services agencies around the world to transform child protection practice and organisation. Andrew has written extensively about safety-organised child protection practice. His most recent book is co-authored with Susie Essex from Bristol, *Working With 'Denied' Child Abuse: The Resolutions Approach*. More information is available at www.signsofsafety.net and www.munroturnellmurphy.com.

Subject Index

Author Index